MW00978073

The Best of
Dot Com
Humor

4018-TURN

The Best of Dot Com Humor

Michael L. Turnbull

4018-TURN

Copyright © 2000 by Michael L. Turnbull.

Library of Congress Number: 00-192895
ISBN #:   Hardcover   0-7388-4981-2
                 Softcover   0-7388-4982-0

All rights reserved. No part of this book may be reproduced or
transmitted in any form or by any means, electronic or mechanical,
including photocopying, recording, or by any information storage
and retrieval system, without permission in writing from the
copyright owner.

This book was printed in the United States of America.

To order additional copies of this book, contact:
Xlibris Corporation
1-888-7-XLIBRIS
www.Xlibris.com
Orders@Xlibris.com

Contents

Dedicated With Love To:

Patty, Danny, Michael, John, Betsy,
Patty F., Danny III, Kara, Murphy,
Karen, Michael Jr., Jack And Jake.

Acknowledgements

Carr.Carr, Ted Mcdirty, Sjhjr, Wrtelp, J.B., Annbos, Capopp6, Dkliv, Hugh M., Onebison, Sjuhasz, Apnichols, Carleurban, Kellerd, The Gentlemen Of The "20", The Gentlemen Of Rolling Rock, All My Internet Friends And Close Personal Friends Who Love A Good Story.

Disclaimer:

A short disclaimer on photos and stories used and their content is as rare as rocking horse manure. Let this book be an exception.

To the best of my knowledge, all jokes used here are part of the public domain. This book is intended for an adult audience and contains some material not appropriate for those under the age of majority.

All reasonable efforts have been made to contact the artist/original copyright holder of each photograph used and obtain permission to use copyright material. Implied permission exists for those photographs that have been injected into the public domain through extensive Internet use.

Chapter One

HOW THE INTERNET HAS CHANGED

THE FACE OF HUMOR

Humor is the second greatest oral tradition in society.(No, Arthur Haley's book *Roots* is not number one.) The Internet's impact on humor mimics its impact on the rest of society-nothing short of dramatic change. Since I come from a business background, let me use the famed "bullet point" format used in memos to discuss how the Internet has affected humor.

- What McDonald's has done for food, the Internet has done for humor. The speed and availability of jokes and stories to net users across the globe is remarkable. I have received by email the same or similar stories from some acquaintances on four different *continents on the same day!* A story that used to take weeks or even months to traverse this country can now cover the globe in minutes. The emphasis on speed is so pervasive in society that a betting man might wager that premature ejaculation may soon be in vogue.

- Like McDonald's, the Internet often does not offer a great deal of variety on its humor menu. To find truly new and original material on the Internet requires a surfer of extraordinary patience and talent. Humor throughout history has always been plagued with this problem. Most stories are surprisingly predictable in nature. The place, time and tone are shifted in the retelling, the central figure is changed, one famous name substituted for another, (President Clinton for Senator Kennedy) but the twist, the punch line, the point remained the same. Even now, with all the changes brought about by the Internet, the impolite answer to the age old query "Have you heard the one about" is still yes.

- The paragraph above notwithstanding, there is a much broader base from which to draw on humor's positive impact because of the Internet. Where we used to rely on the acknowledged experts, Twain, Chaplin, Fields, Marx, Burns, Hope, Skelton, Benney, E.B. White, Parker, Thurber, Benchley, Seinfeld, Robin Williams et al to originate and entertain us through their humor, material that rivals the icons just mentioned flows from the Internet fountain every day. The problem is the Internet is zoned like the state of Florida, the "Palm Beach" mansions of humor are haphazardly deposited among too many "Riviera Beach" doublewide trailers of dubious value. In trying to come up with fifty sites that were truly humorous for you to visit, I had to sift through over ten thousand sites that couldn't bring a smile to the face of a dentist's patient given too much laughing gas.

- A discussion of the Internet and humor would not be complete without at least touching on the base nature of much of the material found on the net. Dark humor and sick jokes seem to be the norm, not the exception.

Dialect humor has moved from pointing out the differences among us to shouting out the boorishness or illiteracy in someone else. Rather than blame this on the Internet, I believe it reflects a certain collapse of idealism in society. Humor, as a reflection, becomes more violent and cynical. Irreverence and lack of discipline change our life and our way of reacting to it. Humor, the human safety valves' resultant mood is altered. The question of how to protect our young from this somewhat hurtful humor is too serious an issue to be covered here.

- There are as many people alive today as ever lived. Add to that fact that a vast number of those people can communicate with each other through the common medium of the Internet. It is inevitable that life will become more full of idea interchanges. Many talented and inspired comic geniuses from all walks of life will converge on this great communication vehicle and diffuse the many different tensions created by this world-wide opportunity.

- Just at a time when we should be most concerned about the proposition that humor should be a balance between aggression and love, we enter a new era where information and communication supercede industrialization just as the industrial age had supplanted the agrarian society. There is now no such thing as the compaction of comic consciousness in this new world. This dispersion will again encourage the multiple approaches that are so important to regenerate humor. Humor thrives in a mixed, plural society and the Internet requires that approach today.

Redneck swimming pool

Chapter Two

SQUEAKY CLEAN

Subject: Feeling old yet?

Just in case you weren't feeling too old today, this will certainly change things.

Each year the staff at Beloit College in Wisconsin puts together a list to try to give the faculty a sense of the mindset of that year's incoming freshmen. Here's this year's list:

1. The people who are starting college this fall across the nation were born after 1980.
2. They have no meaningful recollection of the Reagan Era and did not know he had ever been shot.
3. They were prepubescent when the Persian Gulf War was waged.
4. Black Monday 1987 is as significant to them as the Great Depression.

5. There has been only one Pope. They can only really re-member one president.

6. They were 11 when the Soviet Union broke apart and do not remember the Cold War.

7. They have never feared a nuclear war. "The Day After" is a pill to them, not a movie.

8. They are too young to remember the space shuttle blow-ing up, and Tiananmen Square means nothing to them.

9. Their lifetime has always included AIDS.

10. They never had a polio shot, and likely do not know what it is.

11. Bottle caps have not only always been screw off, but have always been plastic. They have no idea what a pull-top can looks like.

12. Atari pre-dates them, as do vinyl albums.

13. The expression "you sound like a broken record" means nothing to them.

14. They have never owned a record player.

15. They have likely never played Pac Man and have never heard of Pong.

16. Star Wars look very fake to them, and the special effects are pathetic.

17. There have always been red M&Ms, and blue ones are not new. What do you mean there used to be beige ones?

18. They may have heard of an 8-track, but chances are they probably never have actually seen or heard one.

19. The Compact Disc was introduced when they were 1 year old.

20. As far as they know, stamps have always cost about 32 cents.

21. They have always had an answering machine.

22. Most have never seen a TV set with only 13 channels, nor have they seen a black-and-white TV.

23. They have always had cable.

24. There have always been VCRs, but they have no idea what BETA is.

25. They cannot fathom not having a remote control.
26. They were born the year that Walkmen were introduced by Sony.
27. Roller-skating has always meant inline for them.
28. The Tonight Show has always been with Jay Leno.
29. They have no idea when or why Jordache jeans were cool.
30. Popcorn has always been cooked in a microwave.
31. They have never seen Larry Bird play, and Kareem Abdul-Jabbar is a football player.
32. They never took a swim and thought about Jaws.
33. The Vietnam War is as ancient history to them as WWI, WWII, or even the Civil War.
34. They have no idea that Americans were ever held hostage in Iran.
35. They can't imagine what hard contact lenses are.
36. They don't know who Mork was or where he was from.
37. They never heard the terms: "Where's the beef?", "I'd walk a mile for a Camel," or "de plane, de plane!"
38. They do not care who shot J.R. and have no idea who J.R. is.
39. The Titanic was found? I thought we always knew where it was.
40. Michael Jackson has always been white.
41. Kansas, Chicago, Boston, America, and Alabama are places, not groups.
42. McDonald's never came in Styrofoam containers.
43. There has always been MTV.

Subject: Random Thoughts

Does the little mermaid wear an algebra?
If a pig loses its voice, is it disgruntled?
Why do women wear evening gowns to night clubs? Shouldn't they be wearing night gowns?
If love is blind, why is lingerie so popular?
Why is it that when we bounce a check, the bank charges us more of what they already know we don't have any of?

When someone asks you, "A penny for your thoughts," and you put your two cents in, what happens to the other penny?

Why is the man who invests all your money called a broker?

Why do croutons come in airtight packages? It's just stale bread to begin with.

When cheese gets it's picture taken, what does it say?

If you mixed vodka with orange juice and milk of magnesia, would you get a Phillip's Screwdriver?

Why is a person who plays the piano called a pianist, but a person who drives a race car not called a racist?

Why can't you make another word using all the letters in "anagram"?

Why is it that no word in the English language rhymes with month, orange, silver, or purple?

Why, when I wind up my watch, I start it, but when I wind up a project, I end it?

Why is it that we recite at a play and play at a recital?

Why are a wise man and a wise guy opposites?

Why do we say something is out of whack? What is a whack?

Why don't tomb, comb, and bomb sound alike?

Why do overlook and oversee mean opposite things?

If horrific means to make horrible, does terrific mean to make terrible?

Why isn't 11 pronounced onety one?

"I am." is reportedly the shortest sentence in the English language. Could it be that "I Do." is the longest sentence?

If the singular of GEESE is GOOSE, shouldn't a Portuguese person be called a Portugoose?

Why is a procrastinator's work never done?

If lawyers are disbarred and clergymen defrocked, doesn't it follow that electricians can be delighted, musicians denoted, cowboys deranged, models deposed, tree surgeons debarked and dry cleaners depressed?

Do Roman paramedics refer to IV's as "4's"?

Why is it that if someone tells you that there are 1 billion stars in the universe you will believe them, but if they tell you a wall has wet paint you will have to touch it to be sure?

Are people more violently opposed to fur rather than leather because it's much easier to harass rich women than motorcycle gangs?

If you take an Oriental person and spin him around several times, does he become disoriented?

If people from Poland are called "Poles," why aren't people from Holland called "Holes?"

Subject: She's all yours

A fellow bought a new Mercedes and was out on an interstate for a nice evening drive. The top was down, the breeze was blowing through his hair and he decided to open her up. As the needle jumped up to 80mph he suddenly saw a flashing red and blue light behind him.

"There ain't no way they can catch a Mercedes," he thought to himself and opened her up further.

The needle hit 90, 100, 110 and finally 120 with the lights still behind him. "What am I doing?" he thought and pulled over.

The cop came up to him, took his license without a word and examined it and the car. "I've had a tough shift and this is my last pull over. I don't feel like more paperwork so if you can give me an excuse for your driving that I haven't heard before you can go!"

"Last week my wife ran off with a cop," the man said, "and I was afraid you were the one and you were trying to give her back!"

"Have a nice night", said the officer.

Subject: Random Thoughts-2

- Never raise your hands to your kids. It leaves your groin unprotected.
- I'm not into working out. My philosophy: No pain, no pain.
- I am in shape. Round's a shape!
- I'm desperately trying to figure out why kamikaze pilots wore helmets.
- Ever wonder if illiterate people get the full effect of alphabet soup?
- I always wanted to be somebody, but I should have been more specific.
- Did you ever notice when you blow in a dog's face he gets mad at you? But when you take him in a car he sticks his head out the window.
- Have you ever noticed? Anybody going slower than you is an idiot, and anyone going faster is a maniac.
- You have to stay in shape. My grandmother started walking five miles a day when she was 60. She's 97 today and we don't know where she is.
- The reason most people play golf is to wear clothes they would not be caught dead in otherwise.
- Anytime four New Yorkers get into a cab together without arguing, a bank robbery has just taken place.
- I have six locks on my door all in a row. When I go out, I lock every other one. I figure no matter how long somebody stands there picking the locks, they are always locking three.
- The statistics on sanity are that one out of every four Americans is suffering from some form of mental illness. Think of your three best friends. If they are okay, then it's you.

- Now they show you how detergents take out Bloodstains, a pretty violent image there. I think if you've got a T-shirt with a bloodstain all over it, maybe laundry isn't your biggest problem. Maybe you should get rid of the body before you do the wash.
- I ask people why they have deer heads on their walls. They always say because it's such a beautiful animal. There you go. I think my mother is attractive, but I only have photographs of her.
- A lady came up to me on the street and pointed at my suede jacket. "You know a cow was murdered for that jacket?" she sneered. I replied in a psychotic tone, "I didn't know there were any witnesses. Now I'll have to kill you too."
- Future historians will be able to study at the Gerald Ford Library; the Jimmy Carter Library; the Ronald Reagan Library and the Bill Clinton Adult Bookstore.

Subject: New Van Gogh info.

After much careful research, it has been discovered that the artist, Vincent Van Gogh had many relatives. Among them were:

His obnoxious brother	Please Gogh
His dizzy aunt	Verti Gogh
The brother who ate prunes	Gotta Gogh
The brother who worked at a convenience store	Stopn Gogh
The grandfather car dealer from Yugoslavia.	U Gogh
The brother who bleached his clothes white	Hue Gogh
The cousin from Illinois	Chica Gogh
His magician uncle	Wherediddy Gogh
His Mexican cousin	Amee Gogh

The Mexican cousin's American half brother	Gring Gogh
The nephew who drove a stage coach	Wellsfar Gogh
The constipated uncle	Cant Gogh
The ballroom dancing aunt	Tang Gogh
The bird lover uncle	Flaming Gogh
His nephew psychoanalyst	E Gogh
The fruit loving cousin	Mang Gogh
An aunt who taught positive thinking	Way to Gogh
The little bouncy nephew	Poe Gogh
A sister who loved disco	Go Gogh
And his niece who travels the country	Winne Bay Gogh

Subject: Not Again

An Irishman's been drinking at a pub all night. When he stands up to leave, he falls flat on his face. He tries to stand one more time, but to no avail. Again, he falls flat on his face. He figures he'll crawl outside and get some fresh air and maybe that will sober him up. Once outside, he stands up and, sure enough, he falls flat on his face. The Irishman decides to crawl the four blocks to his home.

When he arrives at the door, he stands up and falls flat on his face. He crawls through the door into his bedroom. When he reaches his bed, he tries one more time to stand up. This time, he manages to pull himself upright but he quickly falls right into bed. He is sound asleep as soon as his head hits the pillow.

He awakens the next morning to his wife standing over him, shouting, "So, you've been out drinking again!"

"Why do you say that?" he asks innocently.

"The pub called. You left your wheelchair there again."

Subject: Airplane Humor

Here are some real examples that have been heard or reported:

1. "There may be 50 ways to leave your lover, but there are only 4 ways out of this airplane . . ."
2. After landing: "Thank you for flying Delta Business Express. We hope you enjoyed giving us the business as much as we enjoyed taking you for a ride."
3. As the plane landed and was coming to a stop at Washington National, a lone voice came over the loudspeaker: "Whoa, big fella. WHOA!"
4. After a particularly rough landing during thunderstorms in Memphis, a flight attendant on a Northwest flight announced: "Please take care when opening the overhead compartments because, after a landing like that, sure as hell everything has shifted."
5. From a Southwest Airlines employee. . . . "Welcome aboard Southwest Flight XXX to YYY. To operate your seatbelt, insert the metal tab into the buckle, and pull tight. It works just like every other seatbelt, and if you don't know how to operate one, you probably shouldn't be out in public unsupervised.
6. In the event of a sudden loss of cabin pressure, margarine cups will descend from the ceiling. Stop screaming, grab the mask, and pull it over your face. If you have a small child traveling with you, secure your mask before assisting with theirs. If you are traveling with more than one small child. pick your favorite.
7. Weather at our destination is 50 degrees with some broken clouds, but we'll try to have them fixed before we arrive. Thank you, and remember, nobody loves you, or your money, more than Southwest Airlines."

8. "Your seat cushions can be used for flotation, and in the event of an emergency water landing, please paddle to shore and take them with our compliments."

9. Once on a Southwest flight, the pilot said, "We've reached our cruising altitude now, and I'm turning off the seat belt sign. I'm switching to autopilot, too, so I can come back there and visit with all of you for the rest of the flight."

10. "Should the cabin lose pressure, oxygen masks will drop from the overhead area. Please place the bag over your own mouth and nose before assisting children or other adults acting like children."

11. "As you exit the plane, make sure to gather all of your belongings. Anything left behind will be distributed evenly among the flight attendants. Please do not leave children or spouses."

12. "Last one off the plane must clean it."

13. And from the pilot during his welcome message: "We are pleased to have some of the best flight attendants in the industry . . . Unfortunately, none of them are on this flight . . . !"

14. Heard on Southwest Airlines just after a very hard landing in Salt Lake City: The flight attendant came on the intercom and said, "That was quite a bump and I know what y'all are thinking. I'm here to tell you it wasn't the airline's fault, it wasn't the pilot's fault, it wasn't the flight attendants 'fault . . . it was the asphalt!"

15. Overheard on an American Airlines flight into Amarillo, Texas, on a particularly windy and bumpy day. During the final approach the Captain was really having to fight it. After an extremely hard landing, the Flight Attendant came on the PA and announced, "Ladies and Gentlemen, welcome to Amarillo. Please remain in your seats with your seatbelts fastened while the Captain taxis what's left of our airplane to the gate!"

16. Another flight attendant's comment on a less than perfect landing: "We ask you to please remain seated as Captain Kangaroo bounces us to the terminal."

17. An airline pilot wrote that on this particular flight he had hammered his ship into the runway really hard. The airline had a policy which required the first officer to stand at the door while the Passengers exited, smile, and give them a "Thanks for flying XYZ airline." He said that in light of his bad landing, he had a hard time looking the passengers in the eye, thinking that someone would have a smart comment. Finally everyone had gotten off except for this little old lady walking with a cane. She said, "Sonny, mind if I ask you a question?" "Why no Ma'am," said the pilot, "what is it?" The little old lady said, "Did we land or were we shot down?"

18. After a real crusher of a landing in Phoenix, the Flight Attendant came on with, "Ladies and Gentlemen, please remain in your seats until Capt. Crash and the Crew have brought the aircraft to a screeching halt against the gate. And, once the tire smoke has cleared and the warning bells are silenced, we'll open the door and you can pick your way through the wreckage to the terminal."

19. Part of a flight attendant's arrival announcement: "We'd like to thank you folks for flying with us today. And, the next time you get the insane urge to go blasting through the skies in a pressurized metal tube, we hope you'll think of us here at US Airways."

Subject: Words of Wisdom

- Amateurs built the ark. Professionals built the Titanic.
- Conscience is what hurts when everything else feels so good.
- Talk is cheap because supply exceeds demand.
- Stupidity got us into this mess—why can't it get us out?

- Love is grand; divorce is a hundred grand.
- Even if you are on the right track, you'll get run over if you just sit there.
- Politicians and diapers have one thing in common. They should both be changed regularly and for the same reason.
- An optimist thinks that this is the best possible world. A pessimist fears that this is true.
- There is always death and taxes; however death doesn't get worse every year.
- People will accept your ideas much more readily if you tell them that Benjamin Franklin said it first.
- It's easier to fight for one's principles than to live up to them.
- I don't mind going anywhere as long as it's an interesting path.
- Anything free is worth what you pay for it.
- Indecision is the key to flexibility.
- It hurts to be on the cutting edge.
- If it ain't broke, fix it till it is.
- I don't get even, I get odder.
- In just two days, tomorrow will be yesterday.
- I always wanted to be a procrastinator, never got around to it.
- Dijon vu—the same mustard as before.
- I am a nutritional overachiever.
- My inferiority complex is not as good as yours.
- I am having an out of money experience.
- I plan on living forever. So far, so good.
- I am in shape. Round is a shape.
- Not afraid of heights—afraid of widths.
- Practice safe eating-always use condiments.
- A day without sunshine is like night.
- I have kleptomania, but when it gets bad, I take something for it.

- If marriage were outlawed, only outlaws would have in-laws.
- I am not a perfectionist. My parents were, though.
- Life is an endless struggle full of frustrations and challenges, but eventually you find a hair stylist you like.
- You're getting old when you get the same sensation from a rocking chair that you once got from a roller coaster.
- One of life's mysteries is how a two pound box of candy can make a woman gain five pounds.
- It's frustrating when you know all the answers, but nobody bothers to ask you the questions.
- The real art of conversation is not only to say the right thing at the right time, but also to leave unsaid the wrong thing at the tempting moment.
- Time may be a great healer, but it's also a lousy beautician.
- Brain cells come and brain cells go, but fat cells live forever.
- Age doesn't always bring wisdom, Sometimes age comes alone.
- You don't stop laughing because you grow old, you grow old because you stopped laughing.
- Life not only begins at forty, it begins to show

Subject: I have a sad announcement to make . . .

Please join me in remembering a great icon. Veteran Pillsbury spokesperson, The Pillsbury Doughboy, died yesterday of a severe yeast infection and complications from repeated pokes to the belly. He was 71.

Doughboy was buried in a lightly greased coffin. Dozens of celebrities turned out, including Mrs. Butterworth, the

California Raisins, Hungry Jack, Betty Crocker, the Hostess Twinkies, Captain Crunch and many others.

The graveside was piled high with flours as longtime friend, Aunt Jemima, delivered the eulogy, describing Doughboy as a man who "Never knew how much he was kneaded." Doughboy rose quickly in show business but his later life was filled with many turnovers. He was not considered a very smart cookie, wasting much of his dough on half-baked schemes. Despite being a little flaky at times he even still, as a crusty old man, he was considered a roll model for millions. Toward the end it was thought he'd raise once again, but he was no tart. Doughboy is survived by his second wife, Play Dough. They have two children and one in the oven . The funeral was held at 3:50 for about 20 minutes.

Subject: Sharing

Be thankful for what you have . . .

The little old couple walked slowly into McDonalds that cold winter evening. They looked out of place amid the young families and young couples eating there that night. Some of the customers looked admiringly at them.

You could tell what the admirers were thinking. "Look, there is a couple who has been through a lot together, probably for 60 years or more!" The little old man walked right up to the cash register, placed his order with no hesitation and then paid for their meal. The couple took a table near the back wall and started taking food off of the tray. There was one hamburger, one order of french fries and one drink.

The little old man unwrapped the plain hamburger and carefully cut it in half. He placed one half in front of his wife. Then he carefully counted out the french fries, divided them in two piles and neatly placed one pile in front of his wife. He took a sip of the drink, his wife took a sip and then set the cup down between them. As the man began to eat his few bites of hamburger the crowd began to get restless. Again you could tell what they were thinking. "That poor old couple. All they can afford is one meal for the two of them." As the man began to eat his french fries one young man stood and came over to the old couples table. He politely offered to buy another meal for the old couple to eat. The old man replied that they were just fine. They were used to sharing everything.

Then the crowd noticed that the little old lady hadn't eaten a bite. She just sat there watching her husband eat and occasionally taking turns sipping the drink. Again the young man came over and begged them to let him buy them something to eat. This time the lady explained that no, they were used to sharing everything together. As the little old man finished eating and was wiping his face neatly with a napkin the young man could stand it no longer. Again he came over to their table and offered to buy some food.

After being politely refused again he finally asked a question of the little old lady. "Ma'am, why aren't you eating. You said that you share everything. What is it that you are waiting for?"

She answered, "the teeth"

Subject: Two Irishmen!

Two men were sitting next to each other at a bar. After awhile one guy looks at the other and says, "I can't help but think from listening to you that you're from Ireland."

The other guy replies proudly, "Yes that I am." The first guy says, "So am I. And where from Ireland might you be?" The other guy says, "I'm from Dublin I am."

The first guy responds, "Sure and begora, and so am I. And what street did you live on in Dublin?" The other guy says, "A lovely little area it was. I lived on McCleary Street in the old central part of town."

The first guy says, "Faith and it's a small world—so did I.

And to what school would you have been going?" The other guy answers, "Well now I went to St. Mary's of course."

The first guy gets rets really excited and says, "So did I! Tell me what year did you graduate?" The other guy answers, "Well now I graduated in 1964."

The first guy exclaims, "The good Lord must be smiling down upon us. I can hardly believe our good luck at winding up in the same bar on this very night. Can you believe it, I graduated from St. Mary's in 1964 my own self."

About this time another guy walks into the bar, sits down and orders a beer. The bartender walks over shaking his head and mutters, "It's going to be a long night tonight. The Murphy twins are drunk again."

Subject: Then and Now

- Then: Long hair Now: Longing for hair.
- Then: Keg Now: EKG.
- Then: Acid rock Now: Acid reflux.
- Then: Moving to California because it's cool. Now: Moving to California because it's hot.
- Then: Watching John Glenn's historic flight with your parents. Now: Watching John Glenn's historic flight with your kids.
- Then: Trying to look like Marlon Brando or Elizabeth Taylor. Now: Trying not to look like Marlon Brando or Elizabeth Taylor.
- Then: Seeds and stems. Now: Roughage.
- Then: Popping pills, smoking joints. Now: Popping joints.
- Then: Our president's struggle with Fidel. Now: Our president's struggle with fidelity.
- Then: Paar. Now: AARP.
- Then: Being caught with Hustler magazine. Now: Being caught by Hustler magazine.

- Then: Killer weed. Now: Weed killer.
- Then: Hoping for a BMW. Now: Hoping for a BM.
- Then: The Grateful Dead. Now: Dr. Kevorkian.
- Then: Getting out to a new, hip joint. Now: Getting a new hip joint.

Subject: Equal Opportunity Employer

A local business was looking for office help. They put a sign in the window saying: "HELP WANTED. Must be able to type, must be good with a computer and must be bilingual. We are an Equal Opportunity Employer."

A short time afterwards, a dog trotted up to the window, saw the sign and went inside. He looked at the receptionist and wagged his tail, then walked over to the sign, looked at it and whined. Getting the idea, the receptionist got the office manager. The office manager looked at the dog and was surprised, to say the least. However, the dog looked determined, so he led him into the office. Inside, the dog jumped up on the chair and stared at the manager.

The manager said, "I can't hire you. The sign says you have to be able to type."

The dog jumped down, went to the typewriter and proceeded to type out a perfect letter. He took out the page and trotted over to the manager and gave it to him, then jumped back on the chair.

The manager was stunned, but then told the dog, "The sign says you have to be good with a computer."

The dog jumped down again and went to the computer. The dog proceeded to demonstrate his expertise with various programs and produced a sample spreadsheet and database and presented them to the manager.

By this time the manager was totally dumbfounded! He looked at the dog and said, "I realize that you are a very intelligent dog and have some interesting abilities. However, I still can't give you the job."

The dog jumped down and went to a copy of the sign and put his paw on the part about being an Equal Opportunity Employer.

The manager said, "Yes, but the sign also says that you have to be bilingual."

The dog looked at him straight in the face and said, "Meow."

Subject: Answering machines

- A is for academics, B is for beer. One of those reasons is why we're not here. So leave a message.
- Hi. This is John: If you are the phone company, I already sent the money. If you are my parents, please send money. If you are my financial aid institution, you didn't lend me enough money. If you are my friends, you owe me money. If you are a female, don't worry, I have plenty of money.
- "Hi. Now you say something."
- "Hi! John's answering machine is broken. This is his refrigerator. Please speak very slowly, and I'll stick your message to myself with one of these magnets."
- "Hello, you are talking to a machine. I am capable of receiving messages. My owners do not need siding, windows, or a hot tub. Their carpets are always clean. They give to charity through their office and do not need any pictures taken. They believe the stock market is a random crapshoot, and the entire insurance industry is one huge scam perpetrated by Mafioso accountants. If you're still with me, leave your name and number and they will get back to you."
- "Hi. I am probably home, I'm just avoiding someone I don't like. Leave me a message, and if I don't call back, it's you."

- "This is not an answering machine: this is a telepathic thought-recording device. After the tone, think about your name, your reason for calling, and a number where you can be reached, and my owner will think about returning your call."
- "Hi, this is George. I'm sorry I can't answer the phone right now. Leave a message, and then wait by your phone until I call you back."
- "If you are a burglar, then we're probably at home cleaning our weapons right now and can't come to the phone. Otherwise, we probably aren't home and it's safe to leave us a message."
- "You're growing tired. Your eyelids are getting heavy. You feel very, sleepy now. You are gradually losing your willpower and your ability to resist suggestions. When you hear the tone you will feel helplessly compelled to leave your name, number, and a message."

Subject: I believe it because it's on the Internet

I was on my way to the post office to pick up my case of free M&M's, (sent to me because I forwarded their e-mail to five other people, celebrating the fact that the year 2000 is "MM" in Roman numerals), when I ran into a friend whose neighbor, a young man, was home recovering from having been served a rat in his bucket of Kentucky Fried Chicken—which is predictable, since as everyone knows, there's no actual chicken in Kentucky Fried Chicken, which is why the government made them change their name to KFC.

Anyway, one day this guy went to sleep and when he awoke he was in his bathtub and it was full of ice and he was sore all over and when he got out of the tub he realized that HIS KIDNEYS HAD BEEN STOLEN.

He saw a note on his mirror that said "Call 911!" but he was afraid to use his phone because it was connected to his computer, and there was a virus on his computer that would destroy his hard drive if he opened e-mail entitled "Join the crew!" He knew it wasn't a hoax because he himself was a computer programmer who was working on software to prevent a global disaster in which all the computers get together and distribute the $250.00 Neiman-Marcus cookie recipe under the leadership of Bill Gates. (It's true—I read it all last week in a mass e-mail from BILL GATES HIMSELF, who was also promising me a free Disney World vacation and $5,000 if I would forward the e-mail to everyone I know.)

The poor man then tried to call 911 from a pay phone to report his missing kidneys, but a voice on the line first asked him to press #90, which unwittingly gave the bandit full access to the phone line at the guy's expense. Then reaching into the coin-return slot he got jabbed with an HIV-infected needle around which was wrapped around a note that said, "Welcome to the world of AIDS."

Luckily he was only a few blocks from the hospital—the one where that little boy who is dying of cancer is, the one whose last wish is for everyone in the world to send him an e-mail and the American Cancer Society has agreed to pay him a nickel for every e-mail he receives. I sent him two e-mails and one of them was a bunch of x's and o's in the shape of an angel (if you get it and forward it to more than 10 people, you will have good luck but for 10 people you will only have OK luck and if you send it to fewer than 10 people you will have BAD LUCK FOR SEVEN YEARS).

So anyway the poor guy tried to drive himself to the hospital, but on the way he noticed another car driving without its lights on. To be helpful, he flashed his lights at him and was promptly shot as part of a gang initiation.

Send THIS to all the friends who send you their junk mail and you will receive 4 green M&Ms, but if you don't, the owner of Proctor and Gamble will report you to his Satanist friends and you will have more bad luck: you will get cancer from the Sodium Laureth Sulfate in your shampoo, your wife will develop breast cancer from using the antiperspirant which clogs the pores under your arms, and the government will put a tax on your e-mails forever. I know this is all true 'cause I read it on the Internet

Subject: Top 10 signs you joined a cheap HMO

10. Annual breast exam conducted at Hooters.
9. Directions to your doctor's office include, "take a left when you enter the trailer park."
8. Tongue depressors taste faintly of Fudgesicle.
7. Only proctologist in the plan is "Gus" from Roto-Rooter.
6. Only item listed under Preventive Care feature of coverage is "an apple a day".
5. Your "primary care physician" is wearing the pants you gave to Goodwill last month.
4. "Patient responsible for 200% of out-of-network charges" is not a typo.
3. The only expense covered 100% is embalming.
2. With your last HMO, your heart medicine pills didn't come in different colors with little "M"'s on them.
1. And the Number 1 sign you've joined a cheap HMO . . . When you ask for Viagra, you get a popsicle stick and duct tape.

Subject: Squeaky clean Jokes

- A turtle is mugged by three snails. When asked by the police to describe what happened, he replied, "I don't know, it happened so fast."
- What did the snail say when he jumped on the turtle's back? "WHEEEEEE"
- Why did the Siamese twins go to England? So the other one could have a chance to drive.

- This man is at work one day when he notices his male co-worker is sporting an earring.
  "How long have you been wearing an earring? "Ever since my wife found it in our bed."
- A bull was not interested in a farmer's cows.
  The vet brought some pills and soon the bull not only was servicing the farmer's cows but broke thru the fence to handle the neighbor's cows. "What are those pills," the neighbor asked? "I don't know," said the farmer, "but they sort of taste like chocolate."
- Today's Stock Market Report: Helium was up, Paper was stationary. Pencils lost a few points. Light switches were off. Diapers remained unchanged. Coca Cola fizzled. Scott Tissue hit a new bottom.

Subject: Worst analogies ever written in a high school essay

- He spoke with the wisdom that can only come from experience, like a guy who went blind because he looked at a solar eclipse without one of those boxes with a pinhole in it and now goes around the country speaking at high schools about the dangers of looking at a solar eclipse without one of those boxes with a pinhole in it.
- She caught your eye like one of those pointy hook latches that used to dangle from screen doors and would fly up whenever you banged the door open again.
- The little boat gently drifted across the pond exactly the way a bowling ball wouldn't fell 12 stories, hitting the pavement like a Hefty Bag filled with vegetable soup.
- From the attic came an unearthly howl. The whole scene had an eerie, surreal quality, like when you're on vacation in another city and "Jeopardy" comes on at 7 p.m. instead of 7:30.

- Her hair glistened in the rain like nose hair after a sneeze
- Her eyes were like two brown circles with big black dots in the center.
- Her vocabulary was as bad as, like, whatever
- He was as tall as a six-foot-three-inch tree.
- The hailstones leaped from the pavement, just like maggots when you fry them in hot grease.
- Long separated by cruel fate, the star-crossed lovers raced across the grassy field toward each other like two freight trains, one having left Cleveland at 6:36 p.m. traveling at 55 mph, the other from Topeka at 4:19 p.m. at a speed of 35 mph.
- The politician was gone but unnoticed, like the period after the Dr. on a Dr Pepper can.
- They lived in a typical suburban neighborhood with picket fences that resembled Nancy Kerrigan's teeth
- John and Mary had never met. They were like two hummingbirds who had also never met.
- The thunder was ominous-sounding, much like the sound of a thin sheet of metal being shaken backstage during the storm scene in a play.
- His thoughts tumbled in his head, making and breaking alliances like underpants in a dryer without Cling Free

Subject: A thermodynamics professor . . .

A thermodynamics professor had written a take home exam for his graduate students. It had one question: "Is Hell exothermic (gives off heat) or endothermic (absorbs heat)? Support your answer with a proof."

Most of the students wrote proofs of their beliefs using Boyle's Law (gas cools off when it expands and heats up when it is compressed) or some variant.

One student, however, wrote the following: "First, we need to know how the mass of Hell is changing in time. So, we need to know the rate that souls are moving into Hell and the rate they are leaving. I think that we can safely assume that once a soul gets to Hell, it will not leave. Therefore, no souls are leaving. As for how many souls are entering Hell, let's look at the different religions that exist in the world today. Some of these religions state that if you are not a member of their religion, you will go to Hell. Since there are more than one of these religions and since people do not belong to more than one religion, we can project that all people and all souls go to Hell. With birth and death rates as they are, we can expect the number of souls in Hell to increase exponentially. Now, we look at the rate of change of the volume in Hell because Boyle's Law states that in order for the temperature and pressure in Hell to stay the same, the volume of Hell has to expand as souls are added.

This gives two possibilities:

1. If Hell is expanding at a slower rate than the rate at which souls enter Hell, then the temperature and pressure in Hell will increase until all Hell breaks loose.

2. Of course, if Hell is expanding at a rate faster than the increase of souls in Hell, then the temperature and pressure will drop until Hell freezes over.

So which is it? If we accept the postulate given to me by Ms. Therese Banyan during my Freshman year, 'That it will be a cold night in Hell before I sleep with you,' and take into account the fact that I still have not succeeded in having sexual relations with her, then 2 cannot be true, and so Hell is exothermic."

This student got the only A.

I✦I   Canada Customs   Agence des douanes
        and Revenue Agency   et du revenu du Canada

        Revenue   Revenu
        Canada   Canada

**REVENUE CANADA
1040 EZ 2 DO - TAX FORM
   New Simplified Tax Form for Your Taxes**

1. **How much money did you make?** $_____

2. **Send it to us.**

                              Canada

Subject: Holmes and Dr. Watson

Sherlock Holmes and Dr Watson went on a camping trip. After a good meal and a bottle of wine they lay down for the night, and went to sleep. Some hours later, Holmes awoke and nudged his faithful friend. "Watson, look up at the sky and tell me what you see."

Watson replied, "I see millions and millions of stars." "What does that tell you?"

Watson pondered for a minute. "Astronomically, it tells me that there are millions of galaxies and potentially billions of planets. Astrologically, I observe that Saturn is in Leo. Horologically, I deduce that the time is approximately a quarter past three. Theologically, I can see that God is all powerful and that we are small and insignificant. Meteorologically, I suspect that we will have a beautiful day tomorrow. What does it tell you?"

Holmes was silent for a minute, then spoke. "Watson, you idiot. Someone has stolen our tent."

Subject: The Old West

A cowboy rode into town and stopped at a saloon for a drink. Unfortunately, the locals had a habit of picking on strangers. When the cowboy finished his drink, he found his horse was gone.

He goes back into the bar, handily flips his gun into the air, catches it above his head without even looking and fires a shot into the ceiling.

"Which one of you sidewinders stole my horse?" he yelled.

No one answered

"I'm gonna have another beer and if my hoss ain't back when I'm done, I'm gonna do what I dun in Texas! And I don't like to do what I dun in Texas."

Some of the locals shifted restlessly.

The cowboy finished his beer, walked outside and his horse was back. The bartender comes out and Asks him while he is mounting his stead, "before you go, what happened in Texas."

The cowboy turned and said, "I had to walk home."

Subject: Jewish Humor

Jewish view of when life begins: The fetus is not considered viable until it graduates from law or medical school.

Q-What did the waiter ask the group of dining Jewish mothers? A-Is anything all right?

Q-Where does the Jewish husband hide money from his wife? A-Under the vacuum cleaner.

Short summary of every Jewish Holiday-They tried to kill us, we won, let's eat.

Jewish telegram: Begin worrying, details to follow.

Subject: Mergers

- Hale Business Systems, Mary Kay Cosmetics, Fuller Brush and W.R. Grace—Hale Mary Fuller Grace

- Polygram Records, Warner Brothers and Keebler Crackers —Polly-Warner-Cracker

- 3M and Goodyear —MMMGood

- Fed Ex and UPS— Fed Up

- Grey Poupon and Docker Pants —Poupon Pants

Subject: Air Tragedy

Poland's worst air disaster occurred today when a small two-seater Cessna plane crash-landed into a cemetery early this afternoon in central Poland. Polish search and rescue workers have recovered 826 bodies so far and expect that number to climb as digging continues into the evening.

Subject: Judgement from Little Johnny

Finding one of her students making faces at others on the playground, Ms. Smith stopped to gently rebuke the child. Smiling sweetly the teacher said, "Johnny, when I was a child, I was told that if I made ugly faces, it would freeze and I would stay like that."

Johnny looked up and replied, "Well, Ms. Smith, you can't say you weren't warned."

Subject: Family Feud

A couple drove several miles down a country road, not speaking. An earlier discussion had led to an argument, and neither wished to concede their position.

As they passed a barnyard full of mules and pigs, the wife sarcastically asked, "Relatives of yours?"

"Yep," the husband replied, "In-laws."

Would you have invested?

Microsoft Corporation, 1978

Chapter Three

SLIGHTLY OBJECTIONABLE

Subject: Drinking can alter your personality

Two men are drinking in a bar at the top of the Empire State Bldg. One turns to the other and says: "You know last week I discovered that if you jump from the top of this building by the time you fall to the 10th floor the winds around the building are so intense that they carry you around the building and back into the window. The bartender just shakes his head in disapproval while wiping the bar.

The 2nd Man says: "What are you a nut? There is no way in hell that works."

1st Man: "No it's true let me prove it to you." So he gets up from the bar, jumps over the balcony, and careens to the street below. When he passes the 10th floor, the high wind whips him around the building and back into the 10th floor window and he takes the elevator back up to the bar.

The 2nd Man tells him: "You know I saw that with my own eyes, but that must have been some sort of one time fluke."

1st Man: "No, I'll prove it again" and again he jumps and hurtles toward the street where the 10th floor wind gently carries him around the building and into the window. Once upstairs he urges his fellow drinker to try it.

2nd Man: "Well what the hell, it works, I'll try it." So he jumps over the balcony, plunges downward, passes the 11th, 10th, 9th, 8th floors. and hits the sidewalk with a 'splat.' Back upstairs the Bartender turns to the other drinker: "You know, Superman, you're a real asshole when you drink."

Subject: Fortune Cookie, Anyone?

Passionate kiss like spider's web, soon lead to undoing of fly.

Virginity like bubble, One prick all gone.

Man who run in front of car get tired. Man who run behind car get exhausted.

Man with hand in pocket feel cocky all day.

Foolish man give wife grand piano, wise man give wife upright organ.

Man who walk thru airport turnstile sideways going to Bangkok.

Man with one chopstick go hungry.

Man who scratches ass should not bite fingernails.

Baseball is wrong, man with four balls cannot walk.

Panties not best thing on earth but next to best thing on earth.

War doesn't determine who is right, War determines who is left.

Man who fight with wife all day get no piece at night.

It take many nails to build crib but one screw to fill it.

Man who stand on toilet is high on pot.

Man who lives in glass house should change clothes in basement.

Crowded elevator smells different to midget.

Subject: The New Funk and Wagnell??

The Washington Post recently held a contest in which readers were asked to supply suggested meanings for various words. The following are some of the winning entries:
Abdicate—v., to give up all hope of ever having a flat stomach.
Esplanade—v., to attempt an explanation while drunk.
Willy-nilly—adj., impotent.
Flabbergasted—adj., appalled over how much weight you have gained.
Negligent—adj., describes a condition in which you absent-mindedly answer the door in your nightie..
Lymph—v., to walk with a lisp.
Gargoyle—n., an olive-flavored mouthwash.
Bustard—n., a very rude Metrobus driver.
Coffee—n., a person who is coughed upon.
Flatulence—n., the emergency vehicle that picks you up after you are run over by a steamroller.

Balderdash—n., a rapidly receding hairline.

Testicle—n., a humorous question on an exam.

Rectitude—n., the formal, dignified demeanor assumed by a proctologist immediately before he or she examines you.

Marionettes—n., residents of Washington who have been jerked around by the mayor.

Oyster—n., a person who sprinkles his conversation with Yiddish sayings..

Circumvent—n., the opening in the front of boxer shorts.

Subject: Spud slut

Two little potatoes are standing on the street corner. How can you tell which one is the prostitute?

It's the one with the little sticker that says IDAHO

Subject: Merry Christmas, Officer.

On Christmas morning a cop on horseback is sitting at a traffic light, and next to him is a kid on his shiny new bike.

The cop says to the kid, "Nice bike you got there. Did Santa bring that."

The kid says, "Yeah."

The cop says, "Well, next year tell Santa to put a tail-light on that bike." The cop then proceeds to issue the kid a $20.00 bicycle safety ticket.

The kid takes the ticket and before he rides off says, "By the way, that's a nice horse you got there. Did Santa bring that to you?"

Humoring the kid, the cop says, "Yeah, he sure did."

The kid says, "Well, next year tell Santa to put the dick underneath the horse, instead of on top".

Subject: Three problems-same solution

Three guys are golfing with the club pro. First guy tees off and hits a dribbler about 60 yards. He turns to the pro and says, "What did I do wrong?"

The pro says, 'Loft"

The next guy tees off and hits a duck hook into the woods. He asks the pro, "What did I do wrong?"

The pro says "Loft".

The third guy tees off and hits a slice into a pond. He asks the pro "What did I do wrong?"

The pro says 'Loft".

As they're walking to their balls, the first guy finally speaks up. He says to the pro, "The three of us hit completely different tee shots, and when we when we asked you what we did wrong you answered the same exact answer each time. What is loft?"

The pro says, "Lack of fucking talent."

Subject: Quick Reads

20. Beauty Secrets by Janet Reno
19. Home Built Airplanes by John Denver
18. How to Get To The Super Bowl By Dan Marino
17. Things I Love About Bill by Hillary Clinton
16. My Life's Memories by Ronald Reagan
15. Things I Can't Afford by Bill Gates
14. Things I Would Not Do For Money—by Dennis Rodman
13. The Wild Years—by Al Gore
12. Amelia Earhart's Guide To The Pacific Ocean
11. America's Most Popular Lawyers
10. Detroit—A Travel Guide
9. Dr. Kevorkian's Collection Of Motivational Speeches
8. Everything Men Know About Women
7. Everything Women Know About Men

6. All The Men I've Loved Before—by Ellen Degeneres

5. Mike Tyson's Guide To Dating Etiquette

4. Spotted Owl Recipes—by The Sierra Club

3. The Amish Phone Directory

2. My Plan To Find The Real Killers—by O. J. Simpson

1. My Book Of Morals—by Bill Clinton

Subject: Life in the double wides

You Know You're Trailer Trash When:

1. The Halloween pumpkin on your front porch has more teeth than your spouse.
2. You let your twelve-year-old daughter smoke at the dinner table in front of her kids.
3. You've been married three times and still have the same in-laws.
4. You think a woman who is "out of your league" bowls on a different night.
5. Jack Daniels makes your list of "Most Admired People."
6. You wonder how service stations keep their restrooms so clean.
7. Anyone in your family ever died right after saying, "Hey, watch this!"
8. You've got more than one brother named 'Darryl.'
9. You think that Dom Perignon is a Mafia leader.
10. Your wife's hairdo was once ruined by a ceiling fan.
11. Your Junior/Senior Prom had a Daycare.
12. You think the last words to The Star Spangled Banner are "Gentlemen, start your engines."
13. You lit a match in the bathroom and your house exploded right off its wheels.
14. You had to remove a toothpick for your wedding pictures.
15. The bluebook value of your truck goes up and down, depending on how much gas it has in it.
16. You have to go outside to get something out of the 'fridge.

17. One of your kids was born on a pool table.
18. Your dad walks you to school because you are both in the same grade.
19. You need one more hole punched in your card to get a freebie at the House of Tattoos.
20. You have flowers planted in a bathroom fixture in your front yard.
21. Ya can't get married to yer sweetheart 'cause there's a law 'gainst it.
22. You dated one of your parents' current spouses in high school.
23. You think loading the dishwasher means getting your wife drunk.
24. Your school fight song is "Dueling Banjos."
25. Your toilet paper has page numbers on it.

Subject: Fastest Gun in the West

Morris, as a young man in the Old West wanted to be the best gunfighter alive. One night as he was sitting in a saloon, he spotted an old man who had the reputation of being the greatest gunfighter in his day. So Morris walked up to the old man and told him his dream.

The old man looked him up and down and said "I have a suggestion that is sure to help."

"Tell me, tell me," said the young man.

"Tie the bottom of your holster lower onto your leg."

"Will that make me a better gunfighter?"

"Definitely," said the old man.

Young Morris did what he was told and drew his gun and shot the bow tie off he piano player.

"Wow, that really helped. Do you have any more suggestions?"

"Yeah, if you cut a notch in the top of your holster where the hammer hits, the gun will come out smoother."

"Will that make me a better gunfighter?"

"It sure will," said the old man.

The young guy did what he was told and drew his gun and shot a cufflink off the piano player.

"This is really helping me. Is there anything else you can share with me?"

"One more thing," said the old man. "Get that can of axle grease over there in the corner and rub it all over your gun."

The young Morris didn't hesitate but started putting the grease on the gun barrel.

"No, the whole gun, handle and everything." Said the old man.

"Will that make me a better gunfighter?"

"No," said the old man, "but when Wyatt Earp gets done playing that piano he's going to shove that gun up your ass, and it won't hurt as much."

Subject: The Law of Gravity

Aging Mildred was a 93 year-old woman who was particularly despondent over the recent death of her husband Earl. She decided that she would just kill herself and join him in death. Thinking that it would be best to get it over with quickly, she took out Earl's old Army pistol and made the decision to shoot herself in the heart since it was so badly broken in the first place. Not wanting to miss the vital organ and become a vegetable, she called her doctor's office to inquire as to just exactly where the heart would be. "On a woman," the doctor said, "your heart would be just below your left breast." Later that night, Mildred was admitted to the hospital with a gunshot wound to her knee.

Subject: Manicure or Pedicure?

Three Labrador Retrievers (chocolate, yellow and black colored) are sitting in the waiting room at the vet's office when they strike up a conversation.

The black lab turns to the chocolate and says, "So why are you here?"

He replies, "I'm a pisser. I piss on everything—the sofa, the drapes, the cat, the kids. But the final straw was last night, when I pissed in the middle of my owner's bed."

The black lab says, "So what is the vet going to do?"

"Gonna give me Prozac", came the reply from the chocolate lab. "All the vets are prescribing it. It works for everything."

He then turns to the yellow lab and asks, "Why are you here?"

The yellow lab says, "I'm a digger. I dig under fences, dig up flowers and trees, I dig just for the hell of it. When I'm inside, I dig up the carpets. But I crossed the line last night when I dug a great big hole in my owner's couch."

"So what are they going to do to you?" the black lab inquired.

"Looks like Prozac for me too", the dejected yellow lab said.

The yellow lab then turns to the black lab and asks what he's at the vet's office for.

"I'm a humper", the black lab says. "I'll hump anything. I'll hump the cat, a pillow, the table, fire hydrants, whatever. I want to hump everything I see. Yesterday, my owner had just gotten out of the shower and was bending down to dry her toes and I just couldn't help myself. I hopped on her back and started humping away."

The yellow and chocolate labs exchange a sad glance and say, "So, Prozac for you too, huh?"

The black lab says, "No, I'm here to get my nails clipped."

Subject: Swimming-Breast Stroke Competition

There was a competition to cross the English channel doing only the breaststroke, and the three women who entered the race were a brunette, a redhead and a blonde.

After approximately 14 hours, the brunette staggered up on the shore and was declared the fastest swimmer. About 40 minutes later, the redhead crawled up on the shore and was declared the second place finisher.

Nearly 4 hours after that, the blonde finally came ashore and promptly collapsed in front of the worried onlookers.

When the reporters asked why it took her so long to complete the race, she replied, "I don't want to sound like I'm a sore loser, but I think those two other girls were using their arms."

Subject: Stand back—we don't know how big this may become

One day when the teacher walked to the black board, she noticed someone had written the word 'penis' in tiny letters. She turned around, scanned the class looking for the guilty face. Finding none, she quickly erased it, and began her class.

The next day she went into the room, and she saw, in larger letters, the word 'penis' again on the black board. Again she looked around in vain for the culprit, but found none, so she proceeded with the day's lesson.

Every morning, for about a week, she went into the classroom and found the same disgusting word written on the board, each day's word larger than the previous day's word.

Finally one day she walked in expecting to be greeted by the same word on the board, but instead, found the words: "The more you rub it, the bigger it gets!

Subject: Tough to get good help

A young man wanted to purchase a gift for his new sweetheart's birthday and as they had not been dating very long, after careful consideration, he decided a pair of gloves would strike the right note: romantic but not too personal.

Accompanied by his sweetheart's younger sister, he went to Nordstrom's and bought a pair of white gloves. The sister purchased a pair of panties for herself. During the wrapping, the clerk mixed up the items and the sister got the gloves and the sweetheart the panties.

Without checking the contents, the young man sealed the package and sent it to his sweetheart with the following note:

"I chose these because I noticed that you are not in the habit of wearing any when we go out in the evening. If it had not been for your sister, I would have chosen the long ones with the buttons but she wears short ones that are easier to remove. These are a delicate shade, but the lady I bought them from showed me the pair she had been wearing for the past three weeks and they are hardly soiled. I had her try yours on for me and she looked really smart. I wish I was there to put them on for you the first time as no doubt other hands will come in contact with them before I have a chance to see you again. When you take them off, remember to blow in them before putting them away as they will naturally be a little damp from wearing. Just think how many times I will kiss them during the coming year!

All my love.

P.S. The latest style is to wear them folded down with a little fur showing.

Subject: Is your golf club like this?

Three women are in a club locker room dressing up to play golf, suddenly, a guy runs through the room wearing nothing but a bag over his head. He passes the first woman, who looks down at his privates.

"Thank goodness!!! He's not my husband," she says.

He passes by the second woman, who also looks down as he's passing.

"He's not my husband either." She says, also not recognizing the unit.

He passes by the third woman, who also looks down as he runs by her. "Wait a minute!!!" she says. "He's not even a member of this club!"

Subject: I can explain

Two weeks ago, it was my 45th birthday, and I wasn't feeling too hot when I got up that morning. Anyway, I went into my breakfast knowing that my wife would be pleasant and say, "Happy B-day and probably have a present for me, but she didn't even say, "Good Morning." I said, "Well, that's a wife for you, the children will remember." The children came into breakfast and didn't say a word.

When I started to the office, I was feeling very low and despondent. As I walked into my office, Janet said, "Good Morning, boss . . . Happy Birthday. Then I felt a little better that someone had remembered.

I worked until noon. About noon she knocked at the door and said, "you know, it's such a beautiful day outside, and it's your birthday. Let's go out to lunch—just you and me." So I said,

"That's the best thing I've heard all day. Let's go."

We went to lunch. We didn't go to the place we usually went to. Instead we went to a little place in the country, which was more private. We had two martinis, and lunch was tremendous. We enjoyed it a lot.

On the way back to the office, she said, "You know, it's such a beautiful day. Do we have to go back to the office?"

I said, "No, I guess not".

She said, "let's go over to my apartment and I'll fix you another martini".

We went to her apartment. We enjoyed another martini and smoked a cigarette.

She said, "If you don't mind, I think I'll go into the bedroom and change into something more comfortable.

At this point, I didn't mind a bit." She went into the bedroom, and in about five minutes she came out of the bedroom carrying a large birthday cake, followed by my wife and children, all singing "Happy Birthday."

And there I sat with nothing on but my socks.

Subject: Suggested State Mottos

Alabama: At Least We're not Mississippi

Alaska: 11,623 Eskimos Can't be Wrong!

Arizona: But It's a Dry Heat

Arkansas: Litterasy Ain't Everything

California: As Seen on TV

Colorado: If You Don't Ski, Don't Bother

Connecticut: Like Massachusetts, Only Dirtier and With Less Character (if possible))

Delaware: We Really Do Like Chemicals in our Water

Florida: Ask Us About Medicare and Our Grandkids

Georgia: Without Atlanta We're Alabama.

Hawaii: Haka Tiki Mou Sha'ami Leeki Toru (Death to Mainland Scum, But Leave Your Money)

Idaho: More Than Just Potatoes . . . Well Okay, We're Not, But The Potatoes Are Real Americans

Illinois: Please Don't Pronounce the "S"

Indiana: For 2 Billion Years We've Been Tidal Wave Free

Iowa: Amazing Things You Can Do With Corn

Kansas: Our Grain Is Not Amber, It Is Brown

Kentucky: Five Million People; Seven Last Names

Louisiana: We're Not All Drunk Cajun Wackos, But That's Our Tourism Campaign

Maine: OK, So It's Cold. Do You Think The Moose Care?

Maryland: A Thinking Man's Delaware

Massachusetts: Our Taxes Are Lower Than Sweden's (For Most Brackets)

Michigan: First Line of Defense From the Canadians

Minnesota: "10,000 Lakes—10,000,000,000,000,000,000,000 Mosquitoes"

Mississippi: Come Feel Better About Your Own State (unless you are from the northeast)

Missouri: Your Federal Flood Relief Tax Dollars at Work

Montana: George Custer Slept Here

Nebraska: Ask About Our State Motto Contest

Nevada: Without Poker and Dice, We'd Be A Territory

New Hampshire: Go Away and Leave Us Alone

New Jersey: You Want a ##$%##! Motto? I Got Yer ##$%##! Motto Right Here!

New Mexico: Lizards Make Excellent Pets

New York: You Have the Right to Remain Silent, You Have the Right to an Attorney . . .

North Carolina: Tobacco is a Vegetable

North Dakota: Lewis and Clark Slept Here

Ohio: How Would You Like To Live Next Door To Michigan?

Oklahoma: Was It Rogers and Sullivan? Or Gilbert and Hart?

Oregon: Spotted Owl . . . It's What's For Dinner

Pennsylvania: Cook With Coal

Rhode Island: April Fool !! We're Not REALLY An Island

South Carolina: We Have Never Actually Surrendered. Long Live Jeff Davis !!

South Dakota: Closer Than North Dakota

Tennessee: The Educashun State

Texas: Si, Hablo Ingles (Yes, I speak English)

Utah: The Chinese Did NOT Pay For Our Olympics

Vermont: Yep

Virginia: Who Says Government Stiffs and Slackjaw Yokels Don't Mix?

Washington: Help! We're Overrun By Nerds and Slackers!

Washington, D.C.: Wanna Be Mayor?

West Virginia: One Big Happy Family—Really!

Wisconsin: Dairy Cows Are Not Sheep. Leave Them Alone!

Subject: The good, the bad, and the ugly

Good: Your hubby and you agree, no more kids
Bad: You can't find your birth control pills
Ugly: Your daughter borrowed them

Good: Your son studies a lot in his room
Bad: You find several porn movies hidden there
Ugly: You're in them

Good: Your husband understands fashion
Bad: He's a cross dresser
Ugly: He looks better than you

Good: Your son's finally maturing
Bad: He's involved with the woman next door
Ugly: So are you

Good: You give the birds and bees talk to your daughter
Bad: She keeps interrupting
Ugly: With corrections

Good: Your wife's not talking to you
Bad: She wants a divorce
Ugly: She's a lawyer

Good: The postman's early
Bad: He's wearing fatigues and carrying an AK47
Ugly: You gave him nothing for Christmas

Subject: Stress Buster

When you have had one of those **take this job and shove it** days, try this: On your way home from work, stop at your pharmacy and go to the section where they have thermometers. You will need to purchase a rectal thermometer made by *Q-Tip. Be very sure that you get this brand. When you get home, lock your doors and disconnect the phone so you will not be disturbed during your therapy. Change to very comfortable clothing, such as a sweatsuit and lie down on your bed. Open the package and remove the thermometer. Place it on the bedside table so that it will not become chipped or broken. Take out the written material that accompanies the thermometer and read it. You will notice in small print the statement that "Every rectal thermometer made by Q-Tip is PERSONALLY tested." Now, close your eyes and repeat out loud five times, "I am so glad I do not work in quality control at the Q-Tip Company."

Subject: There is no reality-only perception

Two little boys are sitting in the living room watching TV with their parents. The Mother looks over at the Father with a wink and a nod toward upstairs. The Mother turns back to the two boys and says, We're going upstairs for a minute. You two stay here and watch TV. We'll be right back, ok?"
The two boys nod OK, and the parents take off upstairs. The oldest of the to boys knows the score and he gets up and tiptoes upstairs. At the top of the stairs, he peeks into his Mom and Dad's bedroom and shakes his head.

Back downstairs he says to his little Brother, "Come up here."

So the two little boys tiptoe up the stairs.

Halfway up, the older brother turns to his younger brother and says, "Now I want you to keep in mind, this is the same woman who used to bust our asses for sucking our thumbs!"

Subject: Pest Control

A woman was having a passionate affair with an inspector from a pest-control company. One afternoon they were carrying on in the bedroom together when the husband arrived home a bit early.

"Quick," said the woman to her lover, "into the closet!"

She bundled him in the closet, stark naked.

The husband, however, became suspicious and after a search of the bedroom found the man in the closet.

"Who the hell are you."

"I'm an inspector from Bugs-B-Gone," said the exterminator.

"What are you doing in there?" the husband asked.

"I'm investigating a complaint about an infestation of moths," the man replied.

"And where are your clothes?" asked the husband.

The man looked down at himself and said, "Those little bastards."

Subject: You get what you pay for

Egypt Air is offering a new flight-$29.95-from JFK to JFK jr.

Subject: Silence is golden

THE TOP 10 THINGS MEN SHOULD NOT SAY OUT LOUD IN VICTORIA'S SECRET

10. Does this come in children's sizes?
9. No thanks, just sniffing.
8. I'll be in the dressing room going blind.
7. Mom will love this.
6. Oh the size won't matter. She's inflatable.
5. No need to wrap it up. I'll eat it here.
4. Will you model this for me?
3. The Miracle What?
This is better than world peace!
2. 45 bucks? You're just gonna end up naked anyway.
1. You'll never get your ass into that!

Subject: Method in his madness

A guy walked into a barber shop and asked "how long before I can get a haircut?"

The barber looked around the shop and said "about 2 hours. "The guy left.

A few days later the same guy stuck his head in the door and asked, "How long before I can get a haircut?"

Again, the barber looked around at a shop full of customers and said, "About 2 hours." The guy left again.

A week later the same guy came in the shop again and asked the same question. The barber looked around the shop and said, "About an hour and a half." Once again the guy left.

This time the barber looked over at a friend and said, "Hey, Bill, I'll give you a free cut if you follow that guy and see where he goes."

In a little while, Bill came back into the shop laughing hysterically.

The barber said, "This must be good. Where did he go when he left here?"

"To your house."

Subject: Customer Relations

For all of you out there who've had to deal with an irate customer, this one is for you. In tribute to those 'special' customers we all love! An award should go to the United Airlines gate agent in Denver for being smart and funny & making her point, when confronted with a passenger who probably deserved to fly as cargo.

A crowded United flight was canceled. A single agent was rebooking a long line of inconvenienced travelers. Suddenly an angry passenger pushed his way to the desk. He slapped his ticket down on the counter and said, "I HAVE to be on this flight and it has to be FIRST CLASS."

The agent replied, "I'm sorry sir. I'll be happy to try to help you, but I've got to help these folks first, and I'm sure we'll be able to work something out." The passenger was unimpressed. He asked loudly, so that the passengers behind him could hear, "Do you have any idea who I am?"

Without hesitating, the gate agent smiled & grabbed her public address microphone. "May I have your attention please?" she began, her voice bellowing throughout the terminal. "We have a passenger here at the gate WHO DOES NOT KNOW WHO HE IS. If anyone can help him find his identity, please come to the gate."

With the folks behind him in line laughing hysterically, the man glared at the United agent, gritted his teeth and swore, F*** you!"

Without flinching she smiled and said, "I'm sorry, sir, but you'll have to stand in line for that, too.

Subject: Bravery

Long ago lived a seaman named Captain Bravo. He was a man's man, who showed no fear in facing his enemies. One day, while sailing the seven seas, a lookout spotted a pirate ship and the crew became frantic. Captain Bravo bellowed, "Bring me my red shirt." The First Mate quickly retrieved the captain's red shirt and while wearing the bright frock he led his mates into battle and defeated the pirates.

Later on, the lookout again spotted not one, but two pirate ships. The captain again howled for his red shirt and once again vanquished the enemy.

That evening, all the men sat around on the deck recounting the day's triumphs and one of the them asked the captain, "Sir, why did you call for your red shirt before battle?"

The captain replied, "If I am wounded in the attack, the shirt will not show my blood and thus, you men will continue to resist, unafraid." All of the men sat in silence and marveled at the courage of such a brave man.

As dawn came the next morning, the lookout once again spotted not one, not two, but TEN pirate ships approaching. The rank and file all stared in worshipful silence at the captain and waited for his usual request Captain Bravo gazed with steely eyes upon the vast armada arrayed against his mighty sailing ship and without fear, turned and calmly shouted "Get me my brown pants!"

Subject: Revenge is sweet

In a city park stood two statues, one female and the other male. These two statues faced each other for many years. Early one morning an angel appeared before the statues and said "Since the two of you have brought enjoyment to many people I am giving you a great gift. I bestow the gift of life. You have 30 minutes to do whatever you desire."

And with that command, the statues came to life. The two statues smiled at each other, ran toward some nearby woods and dove behind some foliage.

The angel smiled to himself as he listened to the two statues giggling, bushes rustling and twigs snapping. After fifteen minutes, the two statues emerged from the bushes, satisfied and smiling.

Puzzled, the angel looked at his watch and asked the statues, "You still have 15 minutes, would you like to continue?"

The male statue looked at the female statue and asked, "Do you want to do it again?"

Smiling, the female statue said, "Sure. But this time YOU hold the pigeon down and I'll shit on its head!"

Subject: Take Us to Your Leader

Two aliens landed in the desert near an abandoned gas station.

They approached a gas pump and one of them said to it, "Greetings, Earthling. We come in peace. Take us to your leader."

The gas pump, of course, did not respond.

The alien repeated the greeting, and still there was no response.

Annoyed by what he perceived as the gas pump's haughty attitude, the alien drew his ray gun and said impatiently, "Greetings, Earthling. We come in peace. How dare you ignore us this way? Take us to your leader, or I will fire."

The other alien shouted to his comrade, "No, you must not anger him . . ."

But before he could finish his warning, the first alien fired. There was a huge explosion that blew both of them 200 meters into the desert, where they landed in a heap.

When they finally regained consciousness the one who fired turned to the other one and said, "What a ferocious creature! It nearly killed us. How did you know it was so dangerous?"

The other alien answered, "If there is one thing I have learned in my travels through the galaxy it is this. . . . If a guy has a penis he can wrap around himself twice and then stick in his own ear, don't mess with him."

Subject: Forgive me Father

"I cannot tell you, Father, because I don't want to ruin her reputation."

"Who was this woman you were with—tell me?"

"Please, I cannot tell you, Father, because I don't want to ruin her reputation."

The priest asked, "Was it Brenda Patty O'Malley?"

"No."

"Was it Mary Patricia Kelly?"

"No."

"Was it Elizabeth Mary Shannon?"

"No."

"Was it Fiona Mary McDonald?"

"No."

"Was it Cathy Moran Morgan?"

"No, Father! I cannot tell you."

The priest finally gave up and said, "Tommy, I admire your perseverance, but you must atone for your sins. Your penance will be three Hail Marys and four Our Father's. Go back to your pew."

Tommy walked back to his pew. His friend, Sean, slid over and whispered, "What happened." "Well, I got three Hail Marys, four Our Fathers, and five good leads."

Subject: Gullible's travels

A couple was golfing one day on a very very exclusive golf course lined with million dollar homes. On the third tee, the husband said, "Honey, be very careful when you drive the ball, don't knock out any windows It'll cost us a fortune to fix."

The wife tee'd up and shanked it right through the window of the biggest house on the course. The husband cringed and said, "I told to watch out for the houses. All right, let's go up there, apologize and see how much its going to cost us."

They walk up, knock on the door, and heard a voice say, "Come on in."

They opened the door and saw glass all over the place and a broken bottle lying on its side in the foyer.

A man on the couch said, "Are you the people that broke the window?"

"Uh yes, sorry about that" the husband replied.

"No, actually I want to thank you. I'm a genie that was trapped for a thousand years in that bottle. You've released me. I'm allowed to grant three wishes. I'll give you each one wish, and I'll keep the last one for myself."

"OK," the husband said. "I want a million dollars a year forever."

"No problem—it's the least I can do. And what do you want, my lovely."

"I want a house in every country of the world," she said.

"Consider it done," the genie said.

"And what's your wish, Genie?" the husband said.

"Well, since I haven't had sex with a woman in a thousand years, my wish is to sleep with your wife."

The husband looked at his wife and said, "Well, we did get a lot of money and all those houses, honey. I guess I wouldn't mind if you don't."

The genie took the wife upstairs and ravished her for

two hours. After he was spent, the genie rolled over, looked at the wife and said, "How old is your husband anyway?"

"35," she said.

"No Shit! And he still believes in genies"

Subject: alcohol at work

Take a beer and send the truck to all of your friends!!!!!!

```
|^^^^^^^^^^^^^^^^^| ||____
| B U D W I S E R | ||'|"\,__.
|_..._..._____===|=||_|__|...,]
"(@)'(@)""""*|(@)*(@)*******(@)
```

25 reasons why alcohol should be served at work . . .

1. It's an incentive to show up.
2. It reduces stress.
3. It leads to more honest communications.
4. It reduces complaints about low pay.
5. It cuts down on time off because you can work with a hangover.
6. Employees tell management what they think, not what management wants to hear.
7. It helps save on heating costs in the winter.
8. It encourages carpooling.
9. Increase job satisfaction because if you have a bad job, who cares.
10. It eliminates vacations because people would rather come to work.
11. It makes fellow employees look better.
12. It makes the cafeteria food taste better.
13. Bosses are more likely to hand out raises when they are wasted.
14. Salary negotiations are a lot more profitable.
15. Suddenly, burping during a meeting isn't so embarrassing.

16. Employees work later since there's no longer a need for a break
17. It makes everyone more open with their ideas.
18. Everyone agrees they work better after they've had a couple of drinks.
19. Eliminates the need for employees to get drunk at lunch.
20. Increases the chance of seeing your boss naked. SCARY!!!!
21. It promotes foreign relations with the former Soviet Union
22. The janitor's closet will finally have a use.
23. Employees no longer need coffee to sober up.
24. Sitting on the copy machine will no longer be seen as gross.
25. Babbling and mumbling incoherently will be common, not just restricted to the higher ups.

Subject: Brotherly Love

A mother was preparing pancakes for her two sons, the older 5 and the younger 3.

The boys began to argue over who would get the first pancake.

Their mother saw the opportunity for a moral lesson.

"If Jesus were sitting here," she said, "he would say 'Let my brother have the first pancake, I can wait.'

Kevin turned to his younger brother and said, "Ryan, you be Jesus!"

Subject: Psychic humor

1200 people attended the recent International Psychic Society conference.
Moderator: "How many attendees believe in ghosts?"
(Over 80% of the hands were raised)

Moderator: "How many have actually seen a ghost?"
(58% of the hands were raised)
Moderator: "How many believe that a ghost can be solid?"
(23% of the hands were raised)
Moderator: "How many have ever physically touched a ghost?"
(3% of the hands were raised)
Moderator: "How many have ever had sex with a ghost?"
(After some pause one lonely hand at the back of the hall went up)
Moderator: "May I ask where you are from, sir?"
Attendee: "I am from Australia."
Moderator: "And you say you've had sex with a ghost?"
Attendee: "Oh sorry! I thought you said "goat."

Subject: A good walk spoiled

It was a sunny Saturday morning on the course, and I was beginning my pre-shot routine, visualizing my upcoming shot, concentrating on my swing mechanics, when a voice came over the clubhouse loudspeaker.

"Would the gentleman on the women's' tee back up to the men's' tee."

I was still deep into my routine, seemingly impervious to the loudspeaker.

Again the announcement, " Would the MAN on the WOMEN'S' tee kindly back up to the men's tees."

I simply ignored the guy and kept concentrating, when once more he yelled "Would the man on the women's' tee back up to the men's' tee,"

Finally, I stopped, turned, looked through the clubhouse window, directly at the person with the microphone, and shouted back, "Would the person in the clubhouse kindly shut the f.—up, and let me play my second shot."

Subject: What's mine is yours

Two guys trying to get in a quick eighteen holes, but there are two terrible lady golfers in front of them hitting the ball everywhere but where it's supposed to go.

The first guy says, "Why don't you go over and ask if we can play through?"

The second guy gets about halfway there and comes back.

The first guy says, "What's wrong?"

He says, "One of them is my wife, and the other one is my mistress."

The first guy says, "That could be a problem. I'll go over." He gets about halfway there and comes back.

The second guy says, "What's wrong?"

The first guy says, "Small world."

Subject: The 2000 Federal Census for Alabama

Last name: _____

First name: (Check appropriate box)
(_) Billy-Bob
(_) Billy-Joe
(_) Billy-Ray
(_) Billy-Sue
(_) Billy-Mae
(_) Billy-Jack

What does everyone call you?
(_) Booger
(_) Bubba
(_) Junior
(_) Sissy
(_) Other_____

Age: ____ (if unsure, guess)

Sex: _____ M _____ F _____ Not sure

Shoe Size: _____ Left _____ Right

Occupation: (Check appropriate box)
(_) Farmer
(_) Mechanic
(_) Hair Dresser
(_) Unemployed
(_) Dirty Politician
(_) Preacher

Spouse's Name:_____

2nd Spouse's Name:_____

3rd Spouse's Name:_____

Lover's Name:_____

Relationship with spouse: (Check appropriate box)
(_) Sister
(_) Brother
(_) Aunt
(_) Uncle
(_) Cousin
(_) Mother
(_) Father
(_) Son
(_) Daughter
(_) Pet

Number of children living in household: _____

Number of children living in shed: _____

Number that are yours: _____

Mother's Name: _____(If not sure,
    leave blank)

Father's Name: _____ (If not sure,
    leave blank)

Education: 1 2 3 4 (Circle highest grade completed)

Do you (_) own or (_) rent your mobile home?
(Check appropriate box)

Total number of vehicles you own: ___
Number of vehicles that still crank: ___
Number of vehicles in front yard: ___
Number of vehicles in back yard: ___
Number of vehicles on cement blocks: ___

Firearms you own and where you keep them:
_____ truck
_____ bedroom
_____ bathroom
_____ kitchen
_____ shed

Model and year of your pickup: 196_

Do you have a gun rack?
(_) Yes (_) No; If no, please explain:

Newspapers/magazines you subscribe to:
(_) The National Enquirer
(_) The Globe
(_) TV Guide

(_) Soap Opera Digest
(_) Rifle and Shotgun

Number of times you've seen a UFO:_____

Number of times in the last 5 years you've seen Elvis:_____
Number of times you've seen Elvis in a UFO:_____

How often do you bathe: (_) Weekly (_) Monthly (_) Not
   Applicable

Color of eyes: Left_____ Right_____

Color of hair: (_) Blond (_) Black (_) Red (_) Brown (_)
   White (_) Clairol

Color of teeth: (_) Yellow (_) Brownish-Yellow (_) Brown (_)
   Black (_) N/A

Brand of chewing tobacco you prefer: (_)Red-Man

How far is your home from a paved road? (_) 1 mile (_) 2
   miles (_)just a whoop-and-a-holler (_) road?

Subject: Bumper Stickers We'd Just Love To See

1. Could you drive any better if I shoved that cell phone up
    your ASS?
2. If you can read this, I can slam on my brakes and sue you
3. Jesus loves you, but everyone else thinks you're an asshole
4. 100,000 sperm and YOU were the fastest?
5. Your gene pool needs a little chlorine.
6. You're just jealous because the voices are talking to me
    and not to you.

7. Don't piss me off! I'm running out of places to hide the bodies.
8. You are depriving some poor village of its IDIOT
9. Forget world peace. Visualize using your turn signal.
10. My Hockey (Lacrosse!!) Mom Can Beat Up Your Soccer Mom
11. Grow your own dope, plant a man
12. All Men Are Animals, Some Just Make Better Pets
13. Some people are only alive because it is illegal to shoot them.
14. I used to have a handle on life, but it broke.
15. WANTED: Meaningful overnight relationship.
16. The more you complain, the longer God makes you live.
17. Out of my mind . . . Back in five minutes
18. Hang up and drive.
19. If you can read this, please flip me back over . . . (seen upside-down)
20. Please tell your pants it's not polite to point
21. GUYS: No shirt, no service. GALS: No shirt, no charge.
22. Impotence: Nature's way of saying "No hard feelings"
23. Heart Attacks . . . God's Revenge For Eating His Animal Friends
24. Boldly going nowhere
25. Your ridiculous little opinion has been noted.
26. Try not to let your mind wander. It is too small to be out by itself.
27. Everyone has a photographic memory, some just don't have film
28. Just because your head is pointed, doesn't mean you're sharp.
29. Some people just don't know how to drive. I call these people "Everybody But Me".
30. Don't like my driving? Then quit watching me.
31. CAUTION—Driver legally blonde
32. You Can't Be First But You Can Be Next

Subject: Ways to Annoy Public Bathroom Stallmate

1. Stick your open palm under the stall wall and ask your neighbor, "May I borrow a highlighter?"
2. Drop a marble and say, "Oh shit! My glass eye!"
3. Say, 'Hmmmm, I've never seen that color before."
4. Grunt and strain real loud for 30 seconds and then drop a cantaloupe into the toilet bowl from a height of 6 feet. Sigh relaxingly.
5. Say, "Now how did that get there?"
6. Say, "Humus. Reminds me of humus."
7. Fill up a large flask with Mountain Dew. Squirt it erratically under the stall walls of your neighbors while yelling, "Whoa! Easy boy!"
8. Using a small squeeze tube, spread peanut butter on a wad of toilet paper and drop the wad under the stall wall of your neighbor. Then say, "Whoops, could you kick that back over here please?"
9. Say, "C'mon Mr. Happy? Don't fall asleep on me."
10. Play a well known drum cadence over and over again on your butt cheeks.
11. Say, "Boy, that sure looks like a maggot."
12. Lower a small mirror underneath the stall wall, adjust it so you can see your neighbor and say, "Peek-a-boo!"
13. Drop a D-cup bra on the floor under the stall wall and sing "Born Free".
14. Say, "CORN? When did I eat corn?"
15. Shout "WHOOO-EEE, That's gonna leave a mark

Subject: Lord to Adam

One day The Lord spoke to Adam. "I've got some good news and some bad news," The Lord said.

Adam looked at The Lord and replied, "Well, give me the good news first."

Smiling, The Lord explained, "I've got two new organs for you, one is called a brain. It will allow you to create new things, solve problems, and have intelligent conversations with Eve. The other organ I have for you is called a penis. It will give you great physical pleasure and allow you to reproduce your now intelligent life form and populate this planet. Eve will be very happy that you now have this organ to give her children."

Adam, very excited, exclaimed, "These are great gifts you have given to me. What could possibly be bad news after such great tidings?" The Lord looked upon Adam and said with great sorrow, "You will never be able to use these two gifts at the same time."

Subject: It's murky under there

A drunk stumbles into a baptismal service one Sunday afternoon down by the river. He proceeds to walk down into the water and stand next to the Preacher.

The minister turns and notices the old drunk and says, "Mister, Are you ready to find Jesus?"

The drunk looks back and says, "Yess, Preacher, I sure am."

The minister then dunks the fellow under the water and pulls him right back up.

"Have you found Jesus?" the preacher asked.

"Nooo, I didn't!" said the drunk.

The preacher then dunks him under for quite a bit longer, brings him up and says, "Now, brother, have you found Jesus?"

"Noooo, I did not Reverend."

The preacher in disgust holds the man under for at least 30 seconds this time, brings him out of the water and says in a harsh tone, "My God, man, have you found Jesus yet?

The old drunk wipes his eyes and says to the preacher . . . "Are you sure this is where he fell in."

Subject: The Proctologist

A doctor walked into a bank. Preparing to endorse a check, he pulled a rectal thermometer out of his shirt pocket and tried to write with it. Realizing his mistake, he looked at the thermometer with annoyance and said, "Well that's great, just great, some asshole's got my pen."

Subject: Who's for dinner

The Forest Service has issued a BEAR WARNING in the National Forests for this summer. They're urging everyone to protect themselves by wearing bells and carrying pepper spray. Campers should be alert for signs of fresh bear activity, and they should be able to tell the difference between Black Bear dung and Grizzly Bear dung. Black Bear dung is rather small and round. Sometimes you can see fruit seeds and/or squirrel fur in it. Grizzly Bear dung has bells in it, and it smells like pepper spray.

Subject: Two Nuns and a Vampire

Two nuns are on vacation in Transylvania. Despite all the warnings to the contrary, they've stayed out after dark. Sure enough, as they're driving along, a vampire flies out of the night and lands on their windshield, hissing and baring his horrible bloody fangs.

"Dear Lord! What shall we do?" cries the first nun.

"Turn on the windshield wipers. Maybe that will break his grip," answers the second nun.

No luck. Now the vampire is wet and angry. He claws at the windshield.

"Now what shall we do?" yells the first nun, getting even more scared.

"Weave the car back and forth. Maybe he'll fall off," says the second nun.

No luck. The vampire is beating on the glass now, and it's starting to crack.

"NOW WHAT!?!?!" cries the first nun.

The second nun tries to remember how to get rid of vampires. She has a sudden flash of insight. "Show him your cross!" she yells, triumphantly.

The second nun sticks her head out the window and yells, "Get off the fucking car, asshole!!"

Subject: Who's colored

Dear white fella,
Couple of things you should know:
When I born, I black
When I grow up, I black
When I go in sun, I black
When I cold, I black
When I scared, I black
When I sick, I black
And when I die, I still black.
You white fella,
When you born, you pink
When you grow up, you white
When you go in sun, you red
When you cold, you blue
When you scared, you yellow
When you sick, you green
And when you die, you Grey
And you have the balls to call me colored?

Subject: Are you from New York City?

A Frenchman, an Englishman and a New Yorker were captured by cannibals.

The chief comes to them and says, "The bad news is that

now we've caught you and we're going to kill you. We will put you in a pot, cook you, eat you and then we're going to use your skins to build a canoe. The good news is you can choose how to die.

" The Frenchman says, "I take ze sword."chief

The chief gives him a sword, the Frenchman says, "Vive la France!" and kills himself

The Englishman says, "a pistol for me please."

The chief gives him a pistol and the Englishman points it at his head and says, "God save the Queen!" and kills himself.

The New Yorker says, "Gimme a fork."

The chief is puzzled, but he shrugs and gives him a fork.

The New Yorker takes the fork and starts jabbing himself all over—the stomach, the sides, the chest, everywhere. . . There is blood gushing out all over, it's horrible.

The chief is appalled and asks,, "My God, what are you doing?" And the New Yorker responds,,

"So much for your canoe you stupid fuck!"

Subject: Quick learner

A 5 year old and a 4 year old are upstairs in their bedroom. "You know what," says the 5 year old, "I think it's about time we start swearing."

The 4 year old nods his head in approval.

The 5 year old continues, "When we go downstairs for breakfast I'm gonna say 'hell,' and you say 'ass', OK?"

The 4 year old agrees with enthusiasm.

The mother walks into the kitchen and asks the 5 year old what he wants for breakfast. "Aw hell Mom, I guess I'll have some Cheerios."

WHACK! He flies out of his chair, tumbles across the kitchen floor, gets up and runs upstairs crying his eyes out

The Mom looks at the 4 year old and asks with a stern voice, "And what do YOU want for breakfast, young man?"

"I don't know," he blubbers, " but you can bet your ass it won't be Cheerios."

Subject: Boots

A couple are vacationing in the West. Sam always wanted a pair of authentic cowboy boots. Seeing some on sale one day, he buys them, wears them home, walking proudly. He walks into their room and says to his wife, "Notice anything different, Bessie?"

Bessie looks him over, "Nope."

Sam says excitedly "Come on Bessie, take a good look. Notice anything different about me?"

Bessie looks again, "Nope."

Frustrated, Sam storms off into the bathroom, undresses, and walks back into the room completely naked except for his boots. Again he asks, a little louder this time, "Notice anything different?"

Bessie looks up and says "Sam, what's different? Its hanging down today, it was hanging down yesterday, it'll be hanging down again tomorrow."

Furious, Sam yells, "And do you know why it is hanging down, Bessie? It's hanging down because its looking at my new boots!!!"

Bessie replies "Should've bought a hat, Sam."

Subject: Olympic Gold

A man is out shopping and discovers a new brand of Olympic condoms. Clearly impressed, he buys a pack. Upon getting home he announces to his wife the purchase he just made.

"Olympic condoms?", she blurts, "What makes them so special?"

"There are three colors", he replies, "Gold, Silver and Bronze."

"What color are you going to wear tonight?", she asks cheekily.

"Gold of course", says the man proudly.

The wife responds, "Why don't you wear Silver; it would be nice if you came second for a change!"

Subject: First Love

A man picks up a young woman in a bar and convinces her to come back to his hotel. When they are relaxing afterwards, he asks, "Am I the first man you ever made love to?" She looks at him thoughtfully for a second before replying. "You might be," she says. "Your face looks familiar."

Subject: Could not happen to a nicer guy

Dennis Rodman found a bottle on the beach and picked it up.

Suddenly, a female genie rose from the bottle. "Master, may I grant you one wish?" asked the genie with a smile.

"Hey, bitch. Don't you know who I am? I don't need no woman givin' menuttin!" barked Rodman.

The genie pleaded, "But master, I must grant you a wish or I will be returned to this bottle forever."

Dennis thought a moment. Then, grumbling about the inconvenience of it all, he said, "Okay, okay, I wanna wake up with three white women in my bed in the morning, so just do it!" Giving the genie an evil glare, he screamed, "Now leave me alone!

"The annoyed genie said, "So be it!" and disappeared back into the bottle.

The next morning, Rodman woke up in bed with Lorena Bobbitt, Tonya Harding, and Hillary Clinton. His penis was gone, his leg was broken, and he had no health insurance.

Subject: The Magazine

One day Mom was cleaning Junior's room and in the closet she found a Bondage and Discipline magazine. She became very upset. She hid the magazine until her husband came home and showed it to him." Well, what should we do about this."

He thought a moment and said, " Well, I don't think we should spank him."

Subject: Aunt Annie

Aunt Annie was in her eighties. She was much admired for her sweetness and kindness to all. The pastor came to call one afternoon and she welcomed him into her parlor. She invited him to have a seat while she prepared some tea.

As he sat facing her old pump organ, the young minister noticed a cut glass bowl sitting on top of the organ, filled with water. In the water floated a condom. Imagine his shock and surprise! Imagine his curiosity! Still, he did not feel he could mention the strange sight .

When Annie returned with tea and cookies, they began to chat. The pastor tried to stifle his interest about the bowl and its strange occupant but soon he had to ask.

"Aunt Annie," he said, "I wonder if you would tell me about this?" (pointing to the bowl)

"Oh yes," she replied, "isn't it wonderful! I was walking downtown last fall and I found a little package. The directions said to put it on the organ, keep it wet, and it would prevent disease. And you know, I haven't had a cold all winter."

Subject: Pick the Right Mount

A group of 4th and 5th graders, accompanied by two female teachers, went on a field trip to the local racetrack to learn about thoroughbred horses and the supporting industry

When it was time for a bathroom break, it was decided that the girls would go with one teacher and the boys would go with the other. The teacher assigned to the boys was waiting outside the men's room when one of the boys came out and told her that none of them could reach the urinal.

Having no choice, she went inside and began lifting the little boys up by the armpits, one by one.

As she lifted one, she could not help but notice that he was unusually well endowed.

Trying not to stare, the teacher said " You must be in the 5th."

"No, ma'am," he replied. "I'm in the 7th, riding Silver Sunset. I appreciate the lift."

Subject: When in Rome

A guy walked into a bar in Arkansas and ordered a white wine. Everybody sitting around the bar looked up, expecting to see some pitiful Yankee , a proponent of an alternative lifestyle.

The bartender looked at him and said, "You ain't from around here, are ya boy? Where ya from."

The guy said, " I'm from Indiana."

The bartender asked, " What do you do in Indiana."

"I'm a taxidermist."

The bartender demanded, 'What in the hell is a taxidermist?"

"I mount animals."

The bartender grinned and shouted to the whole bar, "It's okay boys, he's one of us."

Subject: Investment Opportunity

The pharmaceutical company, Glaxo, is working on a drug called "Ginko Viagra" When approved, it will help you remember what the fuck you are doing.

Subject: Top Ten Ways to Tell Someone Their Fly is Unzipped

10. The cucumber has left the salad.
9. Sailor Ned's taking a little shore leave.
8. Paging Mr. Johnson, Paging Mr. Johnson.
7. Quasimodo needs to go back in the tower and tend to his bells.
6. Your pod bay door is open, Hal.
5. Mini Me is making a break for the escape pod.
4. Ensign Hanes is reporting a hull breach on the lower deck, Sir.
3. You've got your fly set for Monica instead of Hillary.
2. Our next guest is someone who needs no introduction.
And the Number One Way to Tell Someone Their Fly is Unzipped is
1. I'm talking about Shaft, can you dig it?

Pardon Me, Officer, While I Finish My Beer

Despite the fact that an officer is pointing a gun at him, a passenger from a stopped vehicle decides to finish his beer. Police stopped the vehicle because they thought it was stolen; it wasn't, but another passenger was taken into custody on an outstanding warrant and was also charged with resisting arrest. Five people were in the vehicle, and drinking was obviously occurring, but the police didn't arrest anyone else. The incident occurred in Klamath Falls, Ore., on Wednesday.

Chapter Four

THE GENDER/AGE GAP

Subject: The Devil

One bright, beautiful Sunday morning, everyone in the tiny town of Johnstown got up early and went to the local church. Before the services started, the townspeople were sitting in their pews and talking about their lives, their families, etc.

Suddenly, the Devil himself appeared at the front of the congregation. Everyone started screaming and running for the front entrance, trampling each other in a frantic effort to get away from evil incarnate.

Soon everyone was evacuated from the Church, except for one elderly gentleman who sat calmly in his pew, not moving, seemingly oblivious to the fact that God's ultimate enemy was in his presence. Now this confused Satan a bit, so he walked up to the man and said, "Don't you know who I am?"

The man replied, "Yep, sure do."

Satan asked, "Aren't you afraid of me?" "Nope, sure ain't," said the man.

Satan was a little perturbed at this and queried, "Why aren't you afraid of me?"

The man calmly replied, "Been married to your sister for over 48 years."

Subject: What's another year

After a few years of married life, this guy finds that he is unable to perform anymore. He goes to his doctor, and his doctor tries a few things but nothing works. Finally the doctor says to him, "This is all in your mind", and refers him to a psychiatrist.

After a few visits to the shrink, the shrink confesses, "I am at a loss as to how you could possibly be cured." Finally the psychiatrist refers him to a witch doctor.

The witch doctor says, "I can cure this", and throws some powder on a flame, and there is a bright flash with billowing blue smoke. The witch doctor says, "This is powerful healing but you can only use it once a year! All you have to do is say '123' and it shall rise for as long as you wish!" The guy then asks the witch doctor, "What happens when it's over?" The witch doctor replies, "All you or your partner has to say is 1234' and it will go down. But be warned it will not work again for a year!"

The guy goes home and that night he is ready to surprise his wife with the good news. He is lying in bed with her and says "123", and suddenly he's "standin' tall".

With a puzzled look on her face, his wife turns over and says, "What did you say '123' for?

Subject: Another opinion

When Ralph first noticed that his penis was growing larger and staying erect longer, he was delighted, as was his wife. But after several weeks his penis had grown to nearly twenty inches. Ralph became quite concerned, so he and his wife went to see a prominent urologist. After an initial examination, the physician explained to the couple that, though rare, Ralph's condition could be cured through corrective surgery.

"How long will Ralph be on crutches?" the wife asked anxiously.

"Crutches? Why would he need crutches?" responded the surprised doctor.

"Well," said the wife coldly, "You ARE planning to lengthen Ralph's legs, aren't you?"

Subject: Showering]

How To Shower Like A Woman
1. Take off clothing and place it in sectioned laundry hamper according to lights and darks.
2. Walk to bathroom wearing long dressing gown. If you see your boyfriend/husband along the way, cover up any exposed flesh and rush to bathroom.
3. Look at your womanly physique in the mirror and stick out your gut so that you can complain and whine even more about how you're getting fat.
4. Get in the shower. Look for facecloth, armcloth, legcloth, long loofah, wide loofah and pumice stone.
5. Wash your hair once with Cucumber and Lamfrey shampoo with 83 added vitamins.
6. Wash your hair again with Cucumber and Lamfrey shampoo with 83 added vitamins.

7. Condition your hair with Cucumber and Lamfrey conditioner enhanced with natural crocus oil. Leave on hair for fifteen minutes.

8. Wash your face with crushed apricot facial scrub for ten minutes until red and raw.

9. Wash entire rest of body with Ginger Nut and Jaffa Cake body wash.

10. Rinse conditioner off hair (this takes at least fifteen minutes as you must make sure that it has all come off).

11. Shave armpits and legs. Consider shaving bikini area but decide to get it waxed instead.

12. Scream loudly when your boyfriend/husband flushes the toilet and you lose the water pressure.

13. Turn off shower.

14. Squeegy off all wet surfaces in shower. Spray mold spots with Tilex.

15. Get out of shower. Dry with towel the size of a small African country. Wrap hair in super absorbent second towel.

16. Check entire body for the remotest sign of a zit. Attack with nails/tweezers if found.

17. Return to bedroom wearing long dressing gown and towel on head.

18. If you see your boyfriend/husband along the way, cover up any exposed flesh and then rush to bedroom to spend an hour and a half getting dressed.

How To Shower Like A Man

1. Take off clothes while sitting on the edge of the bed and leave them in a pile on the floor.

2. Walk naked to the bathroom. If you see your girlfriend/ wife along the way, flash her making the "woo" sound.

3. Look at your manly physique in the mirror and suck in your gut to see if you have pecs (no). Admire the size of your dick in the mirror, scratch your balls and smell your fingers for one last whiff

MICHAEL L. TURNBULL

4. Get in the shower.
5. Don't bother to look for a washcloth. (you don't use one)
6. Wash your face
7. Wash your armpits
8. Crack up at how loud your fart sounds in the shower.
9. Wash your privates and surrounding area.
10. Wash your ass, leaving hair on the soap bar.
11. Shampoo your hair (do not use conditioner).
12. Make a shampoo Mohawk.
13. Pull back shower curtain and look at yourself in the mirror.
14. Pee (in the shower).
15. Rinse off and get out of the shower. Fail to notice water on the floor because you left the curtain hanging out of the tub the whole time.
16. Partial dry off.
17. Look at yourself in the mirror, flex muscles. Admire dick size.
18. Leave shower curtain open and wet bath mat on the floor.
19. Leave bathroom light and fan on.
20. Return to the bedroom with towel around your waist. If you pass your girlfriend/wife, pull off the towel, grab your dick, go" Yeah baby" and thrust your pelvis at her.
21. Throw wet towel on the bed. Take 2 minutes to get dressed.

Subject: DNA

A married couple went to the hospital to have their baby delivered.

Upon their arrival, the doctor said he had invented a new machine that would transfer a portion of the mother's labor pain to the FATHER.

He asked if they were willing to try it out. They were both very much in favor of it. The doctor set the pain transfer to

10% for starters, explaining that even 10% was probably more pain that the father had ever experienced before. But as the labor progressed, the husband felt fine and asked the doctor to go ahead and kick it up a notch. The doctor then adjusted the machine to 20% pain transfer. The husband was still feeling fine.

The doctor checked the husband's blood pressure and was amazed at how well he was doing. At this point they decided to try for 50%. The husband continued to feel quite well. Since the pain transfer was obviously helping out the wife considerably, the husband encouraged the doctor to transfer ALL the pain to him. The wife delivered a healthy baby with virtually NO pain.

She and her husband were ecstatic.

When they got home, the mailman was dead on their porch!

Subject: Saving himself

A guy out on the golf course takes a high speed ball right in the crotch. Writhing in agony, he falls to the ground. He finally gets himself to the doctor. He says, "How bad is it doc? I'm going on my honeymoon next week and my fiancé is still a virgin in every way." The doc said , "I'll have to put your penis in a splint to let it heal and keep it straight. It should be okay next week." So he took four tongue depressors and formed a neat little 4-sided bandage and wired it all together. It was an impressive work of art. The guy mentions none of this to his girlfriend. They marry and on their honeymoon night in the motel room, she rips open her blouse to reveal a gorgeous set of breasts. This was the first time he ever saw them. She says, "You are the first, no one has ever touched these breasts." He pulls down his pants, whips it out and says, "Look at this, it's still in the crate!"

Subject: Quel hombre

Virginia walked into a local drugstore and quietly asked the pharmacist:
"Do you have Viagra?"
Pharmacist: "Yes."
Virginia: "Does it work?"
Pharmacist: "Yes."
Virginia: "Can you get it over the counter?"
Pharmacist: "Yes . . . if I take two."

Subject: Happy Anniversary

Three guys were sitting at a bar talking. One was a doctor, one was a lawyer and one was a biker.

After a sip of his martini, the doctor said; "You know, tomorrow is my anniversary. I got my wife a diamond ring and a new Mercedes. I figure if she doesn't like the diamond ring, she will at least like the Mercedes, and she will know that I love her."

After finishing his scotch, the lawyer replied; "Well, on my last anniversary, I got my wife a string of pearls and a trip to the Bahamas. figured if she didn't like the pearls, she would at least like the trip, and she would know that I love her."

The biker then took a big swig from his beer, and said; "Yeah, well, for my anniversary I got my old lady a tee-shirt and a vibrator. I figured if she didn't like the tee-shirt, she could go fuck herself."

Subject: LIFESAVER

Two elderly ladies are sitting on the front porch, doing nothing.

One lady turns and asks, "Do you still get horny?"

The other replies, "Oh sure I do."

The first old lady asks, "What do you do about it?"

The second old lady replies, "I suck a lifesaver."

After a few moments, the first old lady asks, "Who drives you to the beach?"

Subject: They still love us

1. How many honest, intelligent, caring men in the world does it take to do the dishes?

Both of them.

2. Why did the man cross the road?

He heard the chicken was a slut.

3. Why don't women blink during foreplay?

They don't have time.

4. Why does it take 1 million sperm to fertilize one egg?

They don't stop and ask for directions.

5. What do men and sperm have in common?

They both have a one-in-a-million chance of becoming a human being.

6. How does a man show that he is planning for the future?

He buys two cases of beer.

7. What is the difference between men and government bonds?

The bonds mature.

8. Why are blonde jokes so short?

So men can remember them.

9. How many men does it take to change a roll of toilet paper?

We don't know; it has never happened.

10. Why is it difficult to find men who are sensitive, caring and good looking?

They all already have boyfriends.

11. What do you call a woman who knows where her husband is every night?

A widow.

96   MICHAEL L. TURNBULL

12. When do you care for a man's company?
When he owns it.
13. What are a woman's four favorite animals? A mink in the
    closet, a jaguar in the garage, a tiger in the bedroom, and
    an ass to pay for it all.
14. Why are married women heavier than single women?
Single women come home, see what's in the fridge and go to
    bed. Married women come home, see what's in bed and
    go to the fridge.
15. How did Pinocchio find out he was made of wood?
His hand caught fire.
17. How do you get a man to do sit-ups?
Put the remote control between his toes.
18. What did God say after creating man?
I must be able to do better than that.

Subject: Shake, Rattle And Roll

A little old lady, well into her eighties, slowly enters the front
door of an erotic sex shop. Obviously very unstable on her
feet, she shakily hobbles the few feet across the store to the
counter.

Finally arriving at the counter and grabbing it for support, she asks the sales clerk: "D-d-do y-you h-h-have d-d-
dildos?"

The clerk, politely trying not to burst out laughing, replies: "Yes we do have dildos. Actually we carry many models."

The old woman then asks: D-d-do y-y-you h-h-have a-a-a p-
p-pink one, t-t-ten inches-s-s l-l-long a-a-and a-b-bout t-t-two
inches-s-s th-th-thick-k-k?"

The clerk responds, "Yes we do."

"C-c-can y-y-you t-t-tell m-m-me how-w-w t-t-to t-t-turn t-t-
the f-f-fuckin' th-th-thing-g off-f-f

Subject: Men are very sentimental

There were 11 people hanging onto a rope that came down from a helicopter. Ten were men, and one was a woman. They all decided that one person should get off because if they didn't the rope would break and everyone would die. No one could decide who should go, so finally the woman gave a very touching speech about how she would give up her life to save the others because women were used to giving up things for their husbands and children and giving into men. And all of the men started clapping.

Subject: The Lottery

A woman gets home, screeches her car into the driveway, runs into the house, slams the door and shouts at the top of her lungs, "Honey, pack your bags. I won the damn lottery!"

The husband says, "Oh migod! No shit?! What should I pack, beach stuff or mountain stuff?"

The wife yells back, "It doesn't matter, just get the hell out!"

Subject: Oldies sex

Two women were talking about their lives since they had become Nursing Home residents. They both agreed that life was good but one woman, Ethel, said she was rather upset because her sex life had really died out since she and her husband had come to the nursing home. The other women said that her sex life was great! "The secret to great sex is this" the woman told her, when my husband is getting ready for bed, I get undressed, lay on the bed and put both legs behind my head. When he comes out and sees me like that he gets so excited, we have wild sex the rest of the night! Ethel says, "I'm going to try that tonight"

When Ethel's husband is getting ready in the bathroom that night, she takes off all her clothes. Although, it's a struggle, she gets one leg up and behind her head. Pretty soon, she has the other leg behind her head as well. After accomplishing this great feat, Ethel falls backwards and can't move. It's not too long before her husband comes out of the bathroom. With a shocked look on his face, her husband yells "For Gods sake Ethel, comb your hair and put your teeth in, you look like an asshole"

Subject: 1999 World Women's Liberation Conference

At the 1999 World Women's Liberation Conference the first speaker from England stood up: "At last years' conference we spoke about being more assertive with our husbands. Well, after the conference I went home and told my husband that I would no longer cook for him and that he would have to do it himself! After the first day, I saw nothing. After the second day, I saw nothing. But after the third day, I saw that he had cooked a wonderful roast lamb." The crowd cheered.

The second speaker from Russia stood up: "After last years' conference I went home and told my husband that I would no longer do his laundry and that he would have to do it himself. After the first day, I saw nothing. After the second day, I saw nothing. But after the third day, I saw that he had done not only his own washing, but my washing as well." The crowd cheered.

The third speaker was a good Cajun lady from Louisiana, she stood up: "Afta last years' conference, I went home and tole my husband dat I was no longer doin' his cookin', cleanin' or shoppin' and dat he would have to do it for himself. Afta the first day, I saw nuttin'. Afta the second day, I saw nuttin'. But afta the third day, I could see a little bit betta outta my left eye."

Subject: This would be a miracle

A tourist wanders into a back-alley antique shop in San Francisco's Chinatown. Picking through the objects on display he discovers a detailed, life-sized bronze sculpture of a rat. The sculpture is so interesting and unique that he picks it up and asks the shop owner what it costs.

"Twelve dollars for the rat, sir," says the shop owner, "and a thousand dollars more for the story behind it."

"You can keep the story, old man," he replies, "but I'll take the rat."

The transaction complete, the tourist leaves the store with the bronze rat under his arm. As he crosses the street in front of the store, two live rats emerge from a sewer drain and fall into step behind him. Nervously looking over his shoulder, he begins to walk faster, but every time he passes another sewer drain, more rats come out and follow him.

By the time he's walked two blocks, at least a hundred rats are at his heels, and people begin to point and shout. He walks even faster, and soon breaks into a trot as multitudes of rats swarm from sewers, basements, vacant lots, and abandoned cars.

Rats by the thousands are at his heels, and as he sees the waterfront at the bottom of the hill, he panics and starts to run for the bridge.

Making a mighty leap, he jumps up onto a light post, grasping it with one arm while he hurls the bronze rat into San Francisco Bay with the other, as far as he can heave it.

Pulling his legs up and clinging to the light post, he watches in amazement as the seething tide of rats surges over the breakwater into the sea, where they drown.

Shaken and mumbling, he makes his way back to the antique shop.

"Ah, so you've come back for the rest of the story," says the owner.

"No," says the tourist, "but I was wondering if you have any bronze lawyers!"

Subject: Wear a raincoat

A blonde's car breaks down on the Interstate one day. So she eases it over onto the shoulder of the road. She carefully steps out of the car and opens the trunk.

Out jump two men in trench coats who get in position at the rear of the vehicle where they stand facing oncoming traffic and begin opening their coats and exposing themselves to approaching drivers.

Not surprisingly, one of the worst pileups in the history of this highway occurs.

It's not very long before a police car shows up.

The cop, clearly enraged, runs toward the blonde of the disabled vehicle yelling, "What the hell is going on here?"

"My car broke down," says the lady, calmly.

"Well, what are these perverts doing here by the road?!" asks the cop.

And she said . . . "Those are my emergency flashers!" she replied.

Subject: Spelling

After a long illness, a woman died and arrived at the gates of heaven. While waiting for saint peter to greet her, she peeked through the pearly gates. She saw a beautiful table and sitting around it were her parents and others that she had known and loved in her lifetime and had gone on before her.

They saw her and began calling out, "hello! How are you? We've been waiting for you, good to see you."

When saint Peter came by the woman said to him, "this is such a beautiful place, how can I get in?"

"You have to spell a word", said saint peter.

"Which word?" Inquired the woman.

"love", replied saint peter. She correctly spelled the word and saint peter welcomed her into heaven.

Several years later, Saint Peter came to the woman and asked her to fill in for him at the front gate. While serving there one day, the woman's husband appeared at the gates.

"I am surprised to see you", said the woman. "how have you been?"

"Oh! I have been doing pretty well since you died," her husband told her. "I married the beautiful young nurse that took care of you while you were ill." "I won the lottery shortly after your death and was able to quit work." "My new wife and I were able to travel every week to all the most beautiful places in the world."

"We were doing great until yesterday." "we were on a ski trip, I fell, struck my head and now I'm here."

"How do I get in this place, it's very beautiful?" Asked the husband

"You have to spell a word," replied the woman.

"What word?" Inquired the husband

"Czechoslovakia"

Subject: Male Decision Process

A man is dating three women and wants to decide which to marry. He decides to give them a test. He gives each woman a present of $5000 and watches to see what they do with the money.

The first does a total makeover. She goes to a fancy beauty salon, gets her hair done, new make up and buys several new outfits and dresses up very nicely for the man. She tells him that she has done this to be more attractive for him because she loves him so much. The man was impressed.

The second goes shopping to buy the man gifts. She gets him a new set of golf clubs, some new gizmos for his computer, and some expensive clothes. As she presents these gifts, she tells him that she has spent all the money on him because she loves him so much.

Again, the man is impressed.

The third invests the money in the stock market. She earns several times the $5000. She gives him back his $5000 and reinvests the remainder in a joint account. She tells him that she wants to save for their future because she loves him so much. Obviously, the man was impressed.

The man thought for a long time about what each woman had done with the money, and then he married the one with the biggest tits.

Subject: elderly woman drivers

Two elderly women were out driving in a large car. Both could barely see over the dashboard. As they were cruising along they came to an intersection. The stoplight was red but they went on through it.

The woman in the passenger seat thought to herself, I must be losing it. I could have sworn we went through a red light. After a few more minutes, they came to another inter-section and the light was red again. Again she went right through it. This time the woman in the passenger seat was almost sure that the light had been red, but was really con-cerned that she was losing it. She was getting nervous and decided to pay very close attention to the road and the next intersection to see what was going on.

At the next intersection, sure enough, the light was defi-nitely red and they went right through it!

She turned to the other woman and said, "Mildred! Did

you know we just went through three red lights in a row? You could have killed us!"

Mildred turned to her and said, "Oh shit, am I driving?"

Subject: For Better or Worse

A woman was out golfing one day when she hit her ball into the woods. She went into the woods to look for it and found a frog in a trap. The frog said to her, "If you release me from this trap, I will grant you 3 wishes." The woman freed the frog and the frog said, "Thank you, but I failed to mention that there was a condition to your wishes that whatever you wish for, your husband will get 10 times more or better!" The woman said, "That would be okay," and for her first wish, she wanted to be the most beautiful woman in the world. The frog warned her, "You do realize that this wish will also make your husband the most handsome man in the world, an Adonis, that women will flock to." The woman replied, "That will be okay because I will be the most beautiful woman and he will only have eyes for me." So, KAZAM—she's the most beautiful woman in the world! For her second wish, she wanted to be the richest woman in the world. The frog said, "That will make your husband the richest man in the world and he will be ten times richer than you." The woman said, "That will be okay because what is mine is his and what is his is mine." So, KAZAM she's the richest woman in the world! The frog then inquired about her third wish, and she answered, "I'd like a mild heart attack."

Subject: Correct Gender Reference

She is not a babe or a CHICK. She is a BREASTED AMERI-CAN.

She is not a SCREAMER or MOANER. She is VOCALLY APPRECIATIVE.

She is not EASY. She is HORIZONTALLY ACCESSIBLE.

She does not TEASE or FLIRT—She engages in ARTIFI-CIAL STIMULATION.

She is not DUMB—She is a DETOUR OFF THE INFORMA-TION SUPERHIGHWAY.

She has not BEEN AROUND—She is a PREVIOUSLY EN-JOYED COMPANION.

She does not GET YOU EXCITED—She causes TEMPO-RARY BLOOD DISPLACEMENT.

She is not KINKY—She is a CREATIVE CARETAKER.

She does not have a KILLER BODY—She is TERMINALLY ATTRACTIVE.

She is not an AIRHEAD—She is REALITY IMPAIRED.

She does not get DRUNK or TIPSY—She gets CHEMICALLY INCONVENIENCED.

She is not HORNY—She is SEXUALLY FOCUSED.

She does not have BREAST IMPLANTS—She is MEDICALLY ENHANCED.

She does not NAG YOU—She becomes VERBALLY RE-PETITIVE.

She is not a SLUT—She is SEXUALLY EXTROVERTED.

She does not have MAJOR LEAGUE HOOTERS—She is PICTORIALLY SUPERIOR.

She is not a TWO BIT WHORE—She is a LOW COST PROVIDER.

Subject: death humor

Jake was on his deathbed. His wife Susan, was maintaining a vigil by his side. She held his fragile hand, tears ran down her face. Her praying roused him from his slumber. He looked up and his pale lips began to move slightly. "My darling Susan," he whispered. "Hush, my love," she said. "Rest. Shhh. Don't talk." He was insistent. "Susan," he said in his tired voice. "I have something I must confess to you."

"There's nothing to confess," replied the weeping Susan. "Everything's all right, go to sleep " "No, no. I must die in peace, Susan. I slept with your sister, your best friend and your mother."

"I know," she replied. "That's why I poisoned you."

Subject: That's not what I meant

On a transatlantic flight, a plane passes through a severe storm. The turbulence is awful, and things go from bad to worse when one wing is struck by lightning. One woman in particular loses it. Screaming, she stands up in the front of the plane. "I'm too young to die!" she wails. Then she yells, "Well, if I'm going to die, I want my last minutes on Earth to be memorable! I've had plenty of sex in my life, but no one has ever made me really feel like a woman! Well I've had it! Is there ANYONE on this plane who can make me feel like a WOMAN??" For a moment there is silence. Everyone has forgotten their own peril, and they all stare, riveted, at the desperate woman in the front of the plane. Then, a man stands up in the rear of the plane. "I can make you feel like a woman," he says. He's gorgeous. Tall, built, with long, flowing black hair and jet black eyes, he starts to walk slowly up the aisle, unbuttoning his shirt one button at a time. No one moves. The woman is breathing heavily in anticipation as the stranger approaches. He removes his shirt. Muscles ripple across his chest as he reaches her, and extends the arm holding his shirt to the trembling woman, and whispers: "Here, iron this."

Subject: Revenge!!

A woman came home just in time to find her husband in bed with another woman.

With superhuman strength borne of fury, she dragged her husband down the stairs to the garage and put his penis in a vise. She then secured it tightly and removed the handle. Next she picked up a hacksaw.

The husband terrified, screamed, "Stop! Stop! You're not going to . . . to . . . cut it off are you?!"

The wife, with a gleam of revenge in her eye, said, "Nope. You are. I'm going to set the garage on fire."

Subject: Smooth Talker

Bad Day of Golf

A man staggers into an emergency room with two black eyes and a five iron wrapped tightly around his throat. Naturally the doctor asks him what happened.

Well, it was like this, said the man. I was having a quiet round of golf with my wife, when she sliced her ball into a pasture of cows.

We went to look for it, and while I was rooting around I noticed one of the cows had something white at its rear end. I walked over and lifted up the tail, and sure enough, there was my wife's golf ball stuck right in the middle of the cow's butt. That's when I made my mistake.

"What did you do?" asks the doctor.

Well, I lifted the tail and yelled to my wife, "Hey, this looks like yours!"

Subject: How To Talk About "Most" Men and Still Be Politically Correct

He does not have a beer gut. He has developed a Liquid Grain Storage Facility.

He is not quiet. He is a Conversational Minimalist.

He is not stupid. He suffers from Minimal Cranial Development.

He does not get lost all the time. He discovers Alternative Destinations.

He is not balding. He is in Follicle Regression.

He is not a cradle robber. He prefers Generationally Differential Relationships.

He does not get falling-down drunk. He becomes Accidentally Horizontal.

He does not have his head up his butt. He suffers from Rectal-Cranial Inversion.

He is not short. He is Anatomically Compact.

He does not have a rich daddy. He is a Recipient of Parental Asset Infusion.

He does not constantly talk about cars. He has a Vehicular Addiction.

He does not have a hot body. He is Physically Combustible.

He is not unsophisticated. He is Socially Challenged.

He does not eat like a pig. He suffers from Reverse Bulimia.

He is not a bad dancer. He is Overly Caucasian.

He is not a sex machine. He is Romantically Automated.

He does not hog the blankets. He is Thermally Unappreciative.

He is not a male chauvinist pig. He has Swine Empathy.

He does not undress you with his eyes. He has an Introspective Pornographic Moment.

He is not afraid of commitment. He is Monogamously Challenged.

Subject: Happily married

A groom passes down the aisle of the church to take his place by the altar and the best man notices that the groom has the biggest, brightest smile on his face. The best man says, "Hey man, I know you are happy to be getting married, but what's up—you look so excited."

The groom replies, "I just had the best blow job I have ever had in my entire life and I am marrying the wonderful woman who gave it to me."

Now—the bride comes walking down the aisle and she, too, has the biggest, brightest smile on her face. The maid of honor notices this and says, "Hey, girlfriend, I know you are happy to be getting married, but what's up, you look so excited."

The bride replies "I have just given the last blow job of my entire life."

Subject: The knob

A lady in her late 40's went to a plastic surgeon for a facelift. The doctor told her of a new procedure called "The Knob". This small knob is planted on the back of a woman's head and can be turned to tighten up the skin to produce the effect of a brand new facelift forever. Of course, the woman wanted "The Knob".

Fifteen years later the woman went back to the surgeon with 2 problems.

"All these years everything had been working just fine. I've had to turn the knob on lots of occasions and I've loved the results. But now I've developed two annoying problems. First of all, I've got these terrible bags under my eyes and the knob won't get rid of them."

The doctor looked at her and said, "Don't worry. Those aren't bags, those are your breasts."

She replied, "Well, I guess that explains the goatee."

Subject: Cuckoo Clock

Shortly after I got married, I was invited out for a night "with the boys". I told the wife that I would be home by midnight. Promise! Well, the yarns were being spun and the grog was going down easy, and at around 3 am, drunk as a skunk, I went home. Just as I got in the door, the cuckoo clock started, and cuckooed 3 times.

Quickly I realized she'd probably wake up, so I cuckooed another 9 times. I was really proud of myself for having the presence of mind—even when smashed—to escape a possible conflict.

Next morning the wife asked me what time I got in and I told her 12 o'clock. Whew! Got away with that one! Then she told me that we needed a new cuckoo clock. When I asked why, she said, "Well, it cuckooed 3 times, said 'shit', cuckooed another 4 times, cleared its throat, cuckooed another 3 times, farted, then cuckooed twice more and started giggling."

Subject: Thirty New Seminars For Women

1. The Auto Hood Release, What Is It And Why Is It There
2. Life Beyond Shoes
3. Money, The Non-Renewable Resource
4. How To Get 90 Minutes Out Of An Hour
5. Faking Orgasm: The Moot Point
6. Why Men Don't Like Any Of Your Friends
7. How To Be A Victim Of Marketing
8. How To Get Out Of Bed Without Waking Up Your Man
9. The Yellow Stain or Why You Should Leave The Lid Up
10. Is There Really Enough Makeup In The World
11. How To Get The Most Out Of A Garbage Bag
12. Sex—The Morning Sport
13. Giving Men What They Really Want And Not Making Them Pay For It
14. Cigar Smoke And It's Benefits
15. How To Tell When A Man's Had An Orgasm And What To Do Next
16. Clocks And Time: The Mysterious Connection
17. Tupperware: Its Social And Environmental Drawbacks
18. Where To Look When Your Auto Is In Reverse
19. Learning When Not To Talk, And Then Not Talking

20. How To Avoid Turning Into Your Mother
21. Quality Time: When You And Your Husband Should Spend Time Apart
22. Beyond The Front Page: Exploring The Daily Newspaper
23. How To Accept Criticism or When To Give Up On Cooking
24. How Pornography Can Enhance Your Sex Life
25. Telltales Sounds Associated With Auto Collisions
26. Toilet Paper And The Loss Of The Rain Forests: The Vital Connection
27. Women And Intestinal Gas: Yes, It Can Happen To You
28. When Ignorance Can Be A Blessing: Household Finances And You
29. How To Keep 'Em Guessing, or 101 Ways To Fold A Towel
30. Talking And Driving: There's Got To Be A Way

Subject: Fred & Homer

One day, two old men were in the hallway of their nursing home in their wheelchairs. The nurse approaches the first old man who is making car noises and pretending to drive. "Homer, what are you doing?" asked the nurse. "I'm driving to Florida." replied the man. "Okay. Be careful." said the nurse.

About an hour or so later, the nurse returned and Homer was still pretending to drive. "Where are you now, Homer?" the nursed asked the man. "Almost there" replied the old man.

At that moment, the nurse looked over at the other old man who was jerking off. "What on earth are you doing, Fred?" asked the nurse. Fred replied, "I'm screwing Homer's wife while he's out of town!"

Subject: Diary of a Viagra housewife

Day 1—Just celebrated our 25th anniversary with not much to celebrate. When it came time to reenact our wedding night, he locked himself in the bathroom and cried.

Day 2—Today he told me he has a big secret to tell me. He's impotent, he says, and wants me to be the first to know. Why doesn't he tell me something I **don't** know! I mean, give me a break! He's been dysfunctional for so long, he even walks with a limp!

Day 3—This marriage is in trouble. A woman has needs you know! Sometimes I need something too! Yesterday, I saw a picture of the Washington Monument and burst into tears!

Day 4—A miracle has happened!! There's an new drug on the market that will fix his "problem". It's called Viagra. I told him that if he takes Viagra, things will be just like they were on our wedding night. He asked me if this time I would say HIS name at the "glorious moment".

Day 5—Oh what a glorious morning!! The sun is shining, the birds are singing. My needs have been fulfilled. Everything is perfect.

Day 6—Again!

Day 7—This Viagra thing is going to his head. (No pun intended) Yesterday, at Burger King, the kid behind the counter asked him if he wanted a whopper. He told him, "No thanks. I've already got one."

Day 8—I think he took too many over the weekend. Yesterday, instead of mowing the lawn, he was using his new "friend" as a weed whacker.

Day 9—Okay, I admit it. I'm hiding. I mean, a girl can only take so much. And to make matters worse, he's washing the Viagra down with hard cider! The photo of Janet Reno isn't working anymore. What am I going to do?

Day 10—I'm basically being drilled to death. It's like going out with Black and Decker.

Day 11—I wish he was gay. I've bought him 20 Liza Minelli albums and the Sweatin' to the Oldies tape and he keeps coming after me.

Day 12—Now I know how Saddam Hussein's wife feels. Every time I shut my eyes, there's a sneak attack! It's like going to bed with a scud missile!

Day 13—I've done everything to turn him off. Nothing works. I even started dressing like a nun. He says penguins turn him on.

Day 14—I can't take it anymore. I think I'm going to have to kill him. I just worry about one thing-how will they ever get the lid to close on his casket?

Subject: Carpe Diem

An airline pilot finishes talking to the passengers just after his plane has taken off, and he forgets to turn off the intercom. He says to the co-pilot, "I think I'll go take a dump and then try to screw that new blonde stewardess."

The stewardess hears it, and as she goes running up the aisle to tell him the intercom is still on, she trips on the rug and falls on her ass.

A little old lady looks down at her and says, "There's no rush, honey. He said he had to take a dump first."

Subject: The Perfect Woman would say....

1. I'll swallow it all . . . I love the taste.
2. Are you sure you've had enough to drink?
3. I'm bored. Let's shave my pussy!
4. Oh come on, what do ya say we get a good porno movie, a case of beer, a few joints, and have my friend Tammy over for a threesome!

5. God, if I don't get to blow you soon, I swear I'm gonna bust!
6. I know it's a lot tighter back there but would you please try again?
7. You're so sexy when you're hungover.
8. I'd rather watch football and drink beer with you than go shopping.
9. Let's subscribe to Hustler.
10. Would you like to watch me go down on my girlfriend?
11. Say, let's go down to the mall so you can check out women's asses.
12. I'll be out painting the house.
13. I love it when you play golf on Sunday's, I just wish you had time to play on Saturday too.
14. Honey, our new neighbor's daughter is sunbathing again, come see!
15. I've decided to stop wearing clothes around the house.
16. No, No, I'll take the car to have the oil changed.
17. Your mother did a great job raising you.
18. Do me a favor, forget the stupid Valentine's day thing and buy yourself new clubs.
19. I understand fully . . . our anniversary comes every year for Christ's sake. You go hunting with the guys, it's a wonderful stress reliever.
20. Shouldn't you be down at the bar with your buddies?
21. Christ, not the fucking mall again, come on let's go to that new strip joint!
22. Listen, I make enough money for the both of us, why don't you retire and get that nagging handicap down to 7 or 8.
23. You need your sleep ya big silly, now stop getting up for the night feedings.
24. That was a great fart! Do another one!
25. I signed up for yoga so that I can get my ankles behind my head for ya.

Subject: Camping couple

A couple went on vacation to a fishing resort up north. The husband liked to fish at the crack of dawn; the wife preferred to read.

One morning the husband returned after several hours of fishing and decided to take a short nap. The wife decided to take the boat out. She was not familiar with the lake so she rowed out, anchored the boat, and started reading her book.

Along came the sheriff in his boat, pulled up alongside and said, "Good morning, Ma'am. What are you doing?" "Reading my book," she replied as she thought to herself, "Is this guy blind or what?"

"You're in a restricted fishing area," he informed her. "But, Officer, I'm not fishing. Can't you see that?"

"Well, you have all this equipment, Ma'am. I'll have to take you in and write you up."

"If you do that I will charge you with rape," snapped the irate woman.

"I didn't even touch you," groused the sheriff.

"Yes, that's true . . . but you have all the equipment."

Subject: Always Wash your hands

A very attractive woman goes up to the bar in a quiet rural pub. She gestures alluringly to the bartender, who comes over immediately. When he arrives, she seductively signals that he should bring his face closer to hers. When he does so, she begins to gently caress his full beard. "Are you the manager?" she asks, softly stroking his face with both hands. "Actually, no", the man replies. "Can you get him for me? I need to speak to him", she says, running her hands beyond his beard and into his hair. "I'm afraid I can't", breathes the bartender.. Is there anything I can do?" "Yes, there is. I need you to give him a message" she continues huskily, popping a couple of fingers into his mouth and allowing him to suck them gently. "What should I tell him?" the bartender manages to say. "Tell him, she whispers, "There is no toilet paper or hand soap in the ladies room."

Subject: Barbara Walters

Barbara Walters had done a story on gender roles in Kuwait several years before the Gulf War, and she noted then that women customarily walked about 10 feet behind their husbands. She returned to Kuwait recently and observed that the men now walked several yards behind their wives. Ms Walters approached one of the women for an explanation. "This is marvelous," she said. "What enabled women here to achieve this reversal of roles?" The Kuwaiti woman replied, "Land mines."

Subject: Unbelievable

1943 Guide to Hiring Women
The following is an excerpt from the July 1943 issue of Transportation Magazine. This was serious and written for male supervisors of women in the work force during World War II—a mere 57 years ago! Obviously, the intent was not to be "funny," but by today's standards, this is hilarious! For those of you with efficiency issues, pay attention to #8.

Eleven Tips on Getting More Efficiency Out of Women Employees: There's no longer any question whether transit companies should hire women for jobs formerly held by men. The draft and manpower shortage has settled that point. The important things now are to select the most efficient women available and how to use them to the best advantage.

Here are eleven helpful tips on the subject from Western Properties:

1. Pick young married women. They usually have more of a sense of responsibility than their unmarried sisters, they're less likely to be flirtatious, they need the work or they wouldn't be doing it, they still have the pep and interest to work hard and to deal with the public efficiently.

2. When you have to use older women, try to get ones who have worked outside the home at some time in their lives. Older women who have never contacted the public have a hard time adapting themselves and are inclined to be cantankerous and fussy. It's always well to impress upon older women the importance of friendliness and courtesy.

3. General experience indicates that "husky" girls—those who are just a little on the heavy side—are more even tempered and efficient than their underweight sisters.

4. Retain a physician to give each woman you hire a special physical examination—one covering female conditions. This step not only protects the property against the possibilities of lawsuit, but reveals whether the employee-to-be has any female weaknesses which would make her mentally or physically unfit for the job.

5. Stress at the outset the importance of time the fact that a minute or two lost here and there makes serious inroads on schedules. Until this point is gotten across, service is likely to be slowed up.

6. Give the female employee a definite daylong schedule of duties so that they'll keep busy without bothering the management for instructions every few minutes. Numerous properties say that women make excellent workers when they have their jobs cut out for them, but that they lack initiative in finding work themselves.

7. Whenever possible, let the inside employee change from one job to another at some time during the day. Women are inclined to be less nervous and happier with change.
8. Give every girl an adequate number of rest periods during the day. You have to make some allowances for feminine psychology. A girl has more confidence and is more efficient if she can keep her hair tidied, apply fresh lipstick and wash her hands several times a day.
9. Be tactful when issuing instructions or in making criticisms. Women are often sensitive; they can't shrug off harsh words the way men do. Never ridicule a woman—it breaks her spirit and cuts off her efficiency.
10. Be reasonably considerate about using strong language around women. Even though a girl's husband or father may swear vociferously, she'll grow to dislike a place of business where she hears too much of this.
11. Get enough size variety in operator's uniforms so that each girl can have a proper fit. This point can't be stressed too much in keeping women happy.

Subject: Sexism in the Military?

This is a transcript of US National Public Radio (NPR) interview between a female broadcaster, and US Army General Reinwald who was about to sponsor a Boy scout Troop visiting his military installation.

FEMALE INTERVIEWER: "So, General Reinwald, what things are you going to teach these young boys when they visit your base?"

GENERAL REINWALD: "We're going to teach them climbing, canoeing, archery, and shooting."

FEMALE INTERVIEWER: "Shooting! That's a bit irresponsible, isn't it?"

GENERAL REINWALD: "I don't see why, they'll be properly supervised on the rifle range."

FEMALE INTERVIEWER: "Don't you admit that this is a ter-
ribly dangerous activity to be teaching children?"

GENERAL REINWALD: "I don't see how, . . . we will be teaching them proper rifle range discipline before they even
touch a firearm."

FEMALE INTERVIEWER: "But you're equipping them to
become violent killers."

GENERAL REINWALD: "Well, you're equipped to be a prostitute, but you're not one, are you?"

The radio went silent and the interview ended.

Subject: 25 Harsh Things To Say To A Naked Guy

1. I've smoked fatter joints than that.
2. Ahhhh, it's cute.
3. Why don't we just cuddle?
4. You know they have surgery to fix that.
5. Make it dance.
6. Can I paint a smiley face on it?
7. Wow, and your feet are so big.
8. It's OK, we'll work around it.
9. Will it squeak if I squeeze it?
10. Oh no, a flash headache.
11. Giggle and point.
12. Can I be honest with you?
13. How sweet, you brought incense.
14. This explains your car.
15. Maybe if we water it, it'll grow.
16. Why is God punishing me?
17. At least this won't take long.
18. I never saw one like that before.
19. But it still works, right?
20. It looks so unused.
21. Maybe it looks better in natural light.
22. Why don't we skip right to the cigarettes?

THE BEST OF DOT COM HUMOR

23. Are you cold?
24. If you get me real drunk first.
25. Is that an optical illusion?

Subject: The unkindest cut of all

One night a man and a woman are both at a bar knocking back a few beers. They start talking and come to realize that they're both doctors. After about an hour, the man says to the woman, "Hey. How about if we sleep together tonight. No strings attached. It'll just be one night of fun." The woman doctor agrees to it.

So they go back to her place and he goes in the bedroom. She goes in the bathroom and starts scrubbing up like she's about to go into the operating room. She scrubs for a good 10 minutes.

Finally she goes in the bedroom and they have sex for an hour or so.

Afterwards, the man says to the woman, "You're a surgeon, aren't you?"

"Yeah, how did you know?"

The man says, "I could tell by the way you scrubbed up before we started."

"Oh, that makes sense", says the woman. "You're an anesthesiologist aren't you?"

"Yeah", says the man, a bit surprised. "How did you know?"

The woman answers, "Because I slept through most of it and didn't feel a thing."

Subject: Overcoming grief

An elderly couple was on a cruise and it was really stormy. They were standing on the back of the boat watching the moon when a wave came up and washed the old woman overboard.

They searched for days but couldn't find her, so the captain sent the old man back to shore with the promise that he would notify him as soon as they found something.

Three weeks went by. Finally the old man got a fax from the boat. It read: Sir, sorry to inform you, we found your wife dead at the bottom of the ocean. We hauled her up to the deck and attached to her very most private part was an oyster and inside it was a pearl worth $50,000 . . . please advise.

The old man faxed back: Send me the pearl and re-bait the trap.

Subject: Horny??

Eighty-year-old Bessie bursts into the rec room of the men's retirement home.

She holds her clenched fist in the air and saucily announces, "Anyone who can guess what's in my hand can have sex with me tonight!!"

A witty, elderly gentleman in the rear shouts out, "An elephant?"

Bessie thinks a minute and says, "Close enough."

Subject: Battle of the Bobbits

The battle of the bobbits southern style!!!!!! THE BATTLE OF THE BOBBITS" (sung to the tune of "THE BEVERLY HILLBILLIES")

Come and listen to a story 'bout a man named John, A poor ex-marine with his little wanker gone. It seems one night after gettin' with the wife, She lopped off his dong with the swipe of a knife.

Penis, that is. Clean cut Missed his nuts.

Well, the next thing you know there's a Ginsu by his side, And Lorena's in the car takin' Willie for a ride. She soon got tired of her purple-headed friend . . . tossed him out the window as she rounded a bend.

Curve, that is. Tossed the nub. In the shrub.

She went to the cops and confessed to the attack, And they called out the hounds just to get his weenie back. They sniffed and they barked and they pointed "over there" to John Wayne's henry that was waving in the air.

Found, that is. By a fence. Evidence.

Now peter and John couldn't stay apart for long, So a dick doc said, "Hey, I can fix that dong!" "A needle and a thread is all we're gonna need" And the whole world waited till they heard that Johnny pee'd.

Whizzed, that is. Straight stream. Even seam.

Well he healed and he hardened and he took his case to court, With a half-assed lawyer cause his assets came up short. They cleared her of assault and acquitted him of rape, And his pecker was the only thing they didn't show on tape.

Video, that is. Unexposed. Case Closed.

Ya'll sleep on your stomachs now, 'ya hear

Subject: Heartwarming

Someone who teaches at a Middle School in Safety Harbor, Florida forwarded the following letter. The letter was sent to the principal's office after the school had sponsored a luncheon for the elderly. This story is a credit to all human kind. Read it and forward it to all those who could use a lift.

Dear Safety Harbor Middle School,

God blesses you for the beautiful radio I won at your recent senior citizen's luncheon. I am 84 years old and live at the Safety Harbor Assisted Home for the Aged. All of my family has passed away. It's nice to know that someone really thinks of me. God blesses you for your kindness to an old forgotten lady. My roommate is 95 and always had her own radio, but would never let me listen to it, even when she was napping. The other day her radio fell off the nightstand and broke into a lot of pieces. It was awful and she was in tears. She asked if she could listen to mine, and I said fuck you.

Sincerely, Edna Johnston

Subject: Must be a Lawyer

A man walks into a bar. He sees a beautiful, well-dressed woman sitting on a bar stool alone.

He walks up to her and says, "Hi there, how's it going tonight?"

She turns to him, looks him straight in the eyes and says, "I'll screw anybody at any time, anywhere—your place or my place, it doesn't matter to me."

The guy raises his eyebrows and says, "No shit, what law firm do you work for?"

Subject: Final Answer

A man and a woman are lying in bed, the man turns to his wife and says, "lets get it on."

She says, "not tonight I have a headache."

He says, "is that your final answer?"

She says, "yes, it is my final answer."

He says, "can I call a friend?"

Subject: The perfect man

The perfect man is gentle
Never cruel or mean

He has a beautiful smile
And keeps his face so clean.

The perfect man likes children
And will raise them by your side

He will be a good father
As well as a good husband to his bride.

The perfect man loves cooking
Cleaning and vacuuming too

He'll do anything in his power
To convey his feelings of love for you.

The perfect man is sweet
Writing poetry from your name

He's a best friend to your mother
And kisses away your pain.

He never has made you cry
Or hurt you In any way

Oh, fuck this stupid poem
The perfect man is gay.

Subject: Quel Hombre-2

Mark decided to propose to Juanita, but prior to her acceptance Juanita had to confess to her man about her childhood
illness.

She informed Mark that she suffered a disease that left
her breasts the maturity of a 12-year-old. He stated that it was
OK because he loved her soooo much.

However, Mark felt this was also the time for him to open
up and admit that he also had a deformity too. Mark looked
Juanita in the eyes and said, "I too had a problem. My penis is

the same size as an infant and I hope you could deal with that once we are married." She said "yes I would marry you and learn to live with your infant size penis."

Juanita and Mark got married and they could not wait for the Honeymoon Mark whisked Juanita off to their hotel suite and they started touching, teasing, holding one another.

As Juanita put her hands in Mark's pants she began to scream and run out of the room. Mark ran after her to find out what was wrong.

She stated to Mark, "you told me your penis was the size of an infant!" Mark said, "yes it is . . . 8 pounds, 7 ounces 19" long!!"

Subject: No love lost

An elderly man was walking through the French country-side, admiring the beautiful spring day, when over a hedgerow he spotted a young couple making love in a field.

Getting over his initial shock he said to himself, "Ah, young love . . . ze spring time, ze air, ze flowers . . . C'est magnifique!", and continued to watch, remembering the good old day's that he'd once enjoyed.

Suddenly he gasped and said, "Mais . . . Sacre bleu! Ze woman she is dead!" before heading off as fast as he could to the town to tell Jean, the police chief.

He arrived at the Police Station, out of breath, and shouted, "Jean . . . Jean . . . zere is zis man, zis woman . . . na-ked in farmer Gaston's field making love."

The police chief smiled and said, "Come, come, Henri you are not so old, remember ze young love, ze spring time, ze air, ze flowers? Ah, L'amour! Zis is OK."

"Mais non! You do not understand, ze woman, she is dead!"

Upon hearing this, Jean, leapt up from his seat, rushed out of the station, jumped on his push-bike, pedaled down to the field, confirmed Henri's story, and pedaled all the way back to call the doctor.

He picked up the telephone and screamed, "Pierre, Pierre! This is Jean, I was in Gaston's field, zere is a young couple naked having sex!"

To which Pierre replied, "Jean, I am a man of science. You must remember . . . it's spring, ze air, ze flowers, Ah, L'amour! Zis is very natural."

Jean, still out of breath, grasped in reply, "NON, you do not understand, ze woman, she is dead!"

Hearing this, Pierre exclaimed, "Mon dieu!" grabbed his black medicine bag, stuffed in his thermometer, stethoscope, and other tools, jumped in his car, and drove like a madman down to Gaston's field.

After carefully examining the participants he drove calmly back to Henri and Jean, who were waiting at the station.

When he got there, went inside, smiled patiently, and said, "Ah, mes amis, do not worry. Ze woman, she is not dead, she is British!"

Subject: Planning for the Future

A wife asks her husband, "Honey, if I died, would you remarry?"

After a considerable period of grieving, I guess I would. We all need companionship."

"If I died and you remarried," the wife asks, "would she live in this house?"

"We've spent a lot of money getting this house just the way we want it. I'm not going to get rid of my house. I guess she would."

"If I died and you remarried, and she lived in this house," the wife asks, "would she sleep in our bed?"

"Well, the bed is brand new, and it cost us $2,000. It's going to last a long time, so I guess she would."

"If I died and you remarried, and she lived in this house and slept in our bed, would she use my golf clubs?"

"Oh, no," the husband replies. "She's left-handed."

Subject: Always wash your hands-2

A man and his wife were at home watching TV and eating peanuts. He'd toss them in the air, then catch them in his mouth. In the middle of catching one, his wife asked a question, and as he turned to answer her, a peanut fell in his ear.

He tried and tried to dig it out but he only pushed it in deeper. After hours of trying they became worried and decided to go to hospital. As they were going out the door, their daughter came home with her date.

After being informed of the problem, their daughter's date said he could get the peanut out. The young man shoved two fingers up the father's nose and told him to blow hard. When the father blew, the peanut flew out. The mother and daughter jumped and yelled for joy.

The young man insisted that it was nothing and the daughter and he went to the kitchen for something to eat.

Once he was gone the mother turned to the father. The mother said, "That's wonderful. Isn't he smart? What do you think he's going to be when he grows older?"

The father replied "From the smell of his fingers, . . . our son in-law!"

Subject: First things first

A 75-year-old man went to his doctor's office to get a sperm count . . . don't ask. The doctor gave the man a jar and said, "Take this jar home and bring me back a semen sample tomorrow."

The next day the 75-year-old man reappeared at the doctor's office and gave him the jar, which was as clean and empty as on the previous day. The doctor asked what happened and the man explained: "Well, doc, it's like this—First I tried with my right hand, but nothing. Then I tried with my left hand, but still nothing.

Then I asked my wife for help. She tried with her right hand, then her left, still nothing. "She even tried with her mouth, first with the teeth in, then with her teeth out, and still nothing.

We even called up Earleen, the lady next door and she tried too, first with both hands, then an arm-pit and she even tried squeez'n it between her knees, but still nothing."

The doctor was shocked! "You asked your neighbor?"

The old man replied, "Yep, but no matter what we tried we still couldn't get the damn jar open!

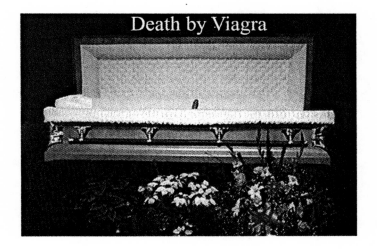

Subject: Don't Lie to Your Mother

John invited his mother over for dinner. During the meal his mother couldn't help noticing how beautiful John's roommate was. She had long been suspicious of a relationship between John and his roommate and this only made her more curious.

Over the course of the evening, while watching the two interact, she started to wonder if there was more between John and the roommate than met the eye. Reading his mom's thoughts, John volunteered, "I know what you must be thinking, but I assure you, Julie and I are just roommates."

About a week later, Julie came to John and said, "Ever since your mother came to dinner, I've been unable to find the beautiful silver gravy ladle. You don't suppose she took it, do you?" John said, "Well, I doubt it, but I'll write her a letter just to be sure."

So he sat down and wrote: "Dear Mother, I'm not saying you 'did' take a gravy ladle from my house, and I'm not saying you 'did not' take a gravy ladle. But the fact remains that one has been missing ever since you were here for dinner"

Several days later, John received a letter from his mother which read: "Dear Son, I'm not saying that you 'do' sleep with Julie, and I'm not saying that you 'do not' sleep with Julie. But the fact remains that if she was sleeping in her own bed, she would have found the gravy ladle by now.
Love,
Mom

Subject: farmer buys a condom

A farmer walked into a drug store and said to the pharmacist, "I want me one of them thar condoms with pesticides on it. Where do I find 'em?"

The pharmacist replied, "Oh sir, you must mean that you want the condoms with SPERMICIDE, not pesticide. They're on aisle 4."

"No, no, I want me them thar condoms with PESTICIDE on it," growled the farmer.

"Sir," said the pharmacist, exasperated from explaining, "PESTICIDE is for killing insects, SPERMICIDE is for killing sperm. I'm sure that you mean spermicide instead of pesticide."

"Listen here," argued the farmer, "I want condoms with PESTICIDE on it, my wife's got a bug up her ass, and I aim to kill it.

Subject: How to Impress a Woman . . .

Wine her,
Dine her,
Call her,
Hug her,
Hold her,
Surprise her,
Compliment her,
Smile at her,
Laugh with her,
Cry with her,
Cuddle with her,
Shop with her,
Give her jewelry,
Buy her flowers,
Hold her hand,
Write love letters to her,
Go the end of the earth and back again for her.

Subject: How to Impress A Man:

Show up naked,
Bring beer.

Subject: 7 Blonde jokes

1. A married couple was asleep when the phone rang at two in the morning, the wife (undoubtedly blonde), picked up the phone, listened a moment and said, "How should I know. That's 200 miles from here!" and hung up.

The husband said, "Who was that?"

The wife said, "I don't know, some woman wanting to know 'if the coast is clear.'

2. Two blondes are walking down the street: One notices a compact on the sidewalk and leans down to pick it up. She opens it; looks in the mirror and says, "Hmm, this person looks familiar."

The second blonde says, "Here, let me see!" So the first blonde hands her the compact. The second one looks in the mirror and says, "You dummy, it's me!"

3. A blonde suspects her boyfriend of cheating on her, so she goes out and buys a gun. She goes to his apartment unexpectedly and when she opens the door she finds him in the arms of a redhead. Well, the blonde is really angry. She opens her purse to take out the gun, and as she does so she is overcome with grief. She takes the gun and puts it to her head.

The boyfriend yells, "No, honey, don't do it."

The blonde replies, "Shut up, you're next!"

4. A blonde was bragging about her knowledge of state capitals. She proudly says,

"Go ahead, ask me, I know all of them."

A friend says, "O.K., what's the capital of Wisconsin?"

The blonde replies, "Oh, that's easy: W."

5. What did the blonde say to her doctor when he told her she was pregnant?

"Is it mine?"

6. A blonde had just totaled her car in a horrific accident. Miraculously, she managed to pry herself from the wreckage without a scratch and was applying fresh lipstick when the state trooper arrived.

"My God!" the trooper gasped. "Your car looks like an accordion that was stomped on by an elephant. Are you OK ma'am?"

"Yes, officer, I'm just fine!" the blonde chirped.

"Well, how in the world did this happen?" the officer asked as he surveyed the wrecked car.

"Officer, it was the strangest thing!" the blonde began. "I was driving along this road when from out of nowhere this TREE pops up in front of me. So I swerved to the right, and there was another tree! I swerved to the left and there was ANOTHER tree! I swerved to the right and there was another tree! I swerved to the left and there was . . ."

"Uh, ma'am", the officer said, cutting her off . . . "there isn't a tree on this road for 30 miles. That was your air freshener swinging back and forth."

7. Returning home from work, a blonde was shocked to find her house ransacked and burglarized. She telephoned the police at once and reported the crime. The police dispatcher broadcast the call on the channels, and a K-9 unit patrolling nearby was the first to respond. As the K-9 officer approached the house with his dog on a leash, the blonde ran out on the porch, shuddered at the sight of the cop and his dog, then sat down on the steps. Putting her face in her hands, she moaned, "I come home to find all my possessions stolen. I call the police for help, and what do they do? They send me a BLIND policeman!"

Subject: Why it's great to be a MAN

- Your ass is never a factor in a job interview.
- Your orgasms are real. Always.
- Your last name stays put.
- The garage is all yours.
- Nobody secretly wonders if you swallow.
- Wedding plans take care of themselves.
- You don't have to curl up next to a hairy ass every night.
- Chocolate is just another snack.
- You can be president.
- You can wear a white shirt to a water park.
- Foreplay is optional.
- You never feel compelled to stop a friend from getting laid.
- Car mechanics tell you the truth.
- You don't give a rat's ass if someone notices your new haircut.
- The world is your urinal.
- Hot wax never comes near your pubic area.
- You never have to drive to another gas station because this one's just too icky.
- Same work . . . more pay.
- Wrinkles add character.
- You don't have to leave the room to make emergency crotch adjustments.
- Wedding Dress $2000; Tux rental $100.
- If you retain water, it's in a canteen.
- People never glance at your chest when you're talking to them.
- Princess Di's death was just another obituary.
- The occasional well-rendered belch is practically expected.
- New shoes don't cut, blister, or mangle your feet.

- Porn movies are designed with you in mind.
- Not liking a person does not preclude having great sex with them.
- Your pals can be trusted never to trap you with: "So, notice anything different?"
- One mood, all the time.

Subject: Smoking

Two old ladies were outside their nursing home, having a smoke, when it started to rain. One of the ladies pulled out a condom, cut off the end, put it over her cigarette, and continued smoking.

Lady 1: What's that? Lady 2: A condom. This way my cigarette doesn't get wet. Lady 1: Where did you get it? Lady 2: You can get them at any drugstore.

The next day, Lady 1 hobbles herself into the local drugstore and announces to the pharmacist that she wants a package of condoms. The guy looks at her kind of strangely (she is, after all, over 80 years of age), but politely asks what brand she prefers.

Lady 1: It doesn't matter as long as it fits a Camel. The pharmacist fainted.

Subject: In sickness and in health

A 92-year-old man moved into a retirement home where he immediately met a 90-year-old woman. They hit if off right away. After a few weeks of spending time together, the man said, "You know, we're past our sexual years, so I wonder if it would be okay for you to just hold my penis in your hand?" The woman answered, "Well, I guess it wouldn't do any harm just to hold it." So, for the next three weeks they could be found on a park bench near a lake, and she was always holding the man's penis in her hand. One day the man didn't show up. Beginning to worry, the lady set out in search of him. A few blocks away, sitting on another park bench was the old man with another woman. The first old lady approached the couple and saw the other woman holding the man's penis in her hand. She became very upset and said to the man, "I thought we had something special. Now I find you with another woman, and she's holding your penis in her hand! What does she have that I don't have?" The old man looked up, smiled, and said, "Parkinson's."

Subject: Husband & Wife

A husband, tired of his wife asking him how she looks, buys her a full-length mirror. This does little to help, as now she just stands in front of the mirror, looking at herself, asking him how she looks. One day, fresh out of the shower, she is yet again in front of the mirror, now complaining that her breasts are too small. Uncharacteristically, the husband comes up with a suggestion. "If you want your breasts to grow, then every day take a piece of toilet paper, and rub it between your breasts for a few seconds." Willing to try anything, the wife fetches a piece of toilet paper, and stands in front of the mirror, rubbing it between her breasts. "How long will this take?" she asks. "They'll grow larger over a period of years," he replies. The wife stops. "Why do you think rubbing a piece of toilet paper between my breasts every day will make my breasts grow over the years?" The husband shrugs. "Why not, it worked for your butt, didn't it?" He lived, and, with a great deal of therapy, he might walk again.

Subject: Grandpa

A man came walking up to the house when he noticed his grandfather sitting on the porch, in the rocking chair, with nothing on from the waist down.

"Grandpa, what are you doing?" he exclaimed. The old man looked off in the distance without answering.

"Grandpa, what are you doing sitting out here with nothing on below the waist?" he asked again.

The old man slowly looked at him and said, "Well, last week I sat out here with no shirt on, and I got a stiff neck. This is your grandma's idea.

Subject: The Golden years

Three men were discussing aging at the nursing home. "Sixty is the worst age to be," said the 60-year-old. You always feel like you have to pee. And most of the time, you stand at the toilet and nothing comes out."

"Ah, that's nothin'," said the 70-year-old. "When you're seventy, you can't even crap anymore. You take laxatives, eat bran, you sit on the toilet all day and nothin' comes out!"

"Actually," said the 80-year-old, "Eighty is the worst age of all."

"Do you have trouble peeing too?" asked the 60-year-old.

"No, not really. I pee every morning at 6:00. I pee like a racehorse on a flat rock; no problem at all. "Do you have trouble crapping?" "No, I crap every morning at 6:30."

With great exasperation, the 60-year-old said, "Let me get this straight. You pee every morning at 6:00 and crap every morning at 6:30. So what's so tough about being 80?"

"I don't wake up until 7:00."

Subject: You're in good hands

Two old ladies sitting on the porch at the old folks home. One turned to the other and asked, "Martha, you were married a long time, did you and your husband have mutual orgasm?"

The other little old lady sat and rocked for a minute and said, "No, I think we had State Farm."

Subject: Behind door number two

Seems God was just about done creating the universe, but he had two extra things left in his bag of creations. So, he decided to split them between Adam and Eve. He told the couple that one of the things he had to give away was the ability to stand up while urinating.

"It's a very handy thing," God told the couple, who he found under an apple tree. "I was wondering if either one of you wanted the ability".

Adam jumped up and blurted, "Oh, give that to me! I'd love to! Please, oh please, oh please, let me have that ability. It'd be so great! When I'm out working in the garden or naming the animals, I could just stand there and let it fly! It'd be so cool, I could write my name in the sand. Oh, please God, let it be me who you give that gift to, let me stand and pee, oh please!!"

On and on he went, like an excited little boy who . . . well . . . had to pee. Eve just smiled and told God that if Adam really wanted that so badly, that he should have it. it seemed to be the sort of thing that would make him happy, and she really wouldn't mind if Adam were the one given this ability. And so, Adam was given the ability to control the direction of his urine while in a vertical position. He was so happy, he celebrated by wetting down the bark on the tree nearest him, laughing with delight all the while.

And it was good. "Fine," God said, looking back into his bag of leftover gifts, "What's left in here?" "Oh yes," he said, "Multiple orgasms . . ."

Subject: bran muffins . . .

This 85-year-old couple, having been married almost 60 years, die in a car crash. They had been in good health the last ten years, mainly due to the wife's neurotic interest in health food.

When they reached the pearly gates, St. Peter took them to their mansion, which was decked out with a beautiful kitchen and master bath suite and Jacuzzi. As they "oohed and aahed", the old man asked Peter how much all this was going to cost.

"It's free," Peter replied, Remember, this is Heaven."

Next they went out back to see the championship golf course the home backed up to. They would have golfing privileges every day, and each week the course changed to a new one representing the great golf courses on Earth.

The old man asked, "What are the green fees?"

"This is heaven," St. Peter replied. "You play for free."

Next they went to the clubhouse and saw the lavish buffet lunch with the cuisine of the world laid out.

"How much to eat?" asked the old man.

"Don't you understand yet?" St. Peter asked. "This is heaven. It's free!"

"Well, where are the low fat and low cholesterol foods?" the old man asked timidly.

"That's the best part . . . you can eat as much as you like of whatever you like and you never get fat and you never get sick. This is Heaven."

The old man looked at his wife and said, "You and your fucking bran muffins. I could have been here ten years ago!"

Subject:—Why Women Talk So Much—

A husband, proving to his wife that women talk more than men, showed her a study which indicated that men use on the average only 15,000 words a day, whereas women use 30,000 words a day. She thought about this for a while and then told her husband that women use twice as many words as men because they have to repeat everything they say.

Looking stunned, he said, "What?"

Subject: Perfect Days

The Perfect Day For A Woman
8:15a—Wake up to hugs and kisses
8:30a—Weigh in 5.1 lbs. lighter than yesterday
8:45a—Breakfast in bed, fresh squeezed orange juice with
    croissants
9:15a—soothing hot bath with fragrant lilac bath oil
10:00a—Light workout with handsome, funny personal
    trainer
10:30a—Facial, manicure, shampoo, and comb out
12:00p—Lunch with best friend at outdoor cafe
12:45p—Notice ex-boyfriends wife, she has gained 30 lbs.
1:00p—Shopping with friends, unlimited credit
3:00p—Nap 4:00p—Three dozen roses delivered, card is
    from secret admirer
4:15p—Light workout at club, followed by gentle massage
5:30p—Pick out outfit for dinner, primp before mirror
6:30p—Candlelight dinner for two followed by dancing
10:00p—Hot shower (alone) 10:30p—Make love
11:00p—Pillow talk, light touching and cuddling
11:30p—Fall asleep in his big, strong arms

The Perfect Day For A Man
6:00a—Alarm
6:15a—Blowjob
6:30a—Massive dump while reading USA Today sports page
7:00a—Breakfast, fillet mignon and eggs, toast and coffee
7:30a—Limo arrives
7:45a—Stoli Bloody Mary enroute to airport
8:15a—Private jet to Augusta, Georgia
9:30a—Limo to Augusta National Golf Club
9:45a—Front nine at Augusta (2 under)
11:45a—Lunch, 2 dozen oysters in the half shell, 3 Heinekens
12:15p—Blowjob

12:30p—Back nine at Augusta (4 under)

2:15p—Limo back to airport (Bombay martini)

3:14p—Fishing excursion with all female crew (topless)

4:30p—Land world record light tackle Marlin (1249 lbs)

5:00p—Jet back and get massage and hand job enroute by Kathy Ireland

6:45p—Shit, shower and shave

7:00p—Watch CNN: Clinton resigns, Hillary and Al Gore farm animal video released

7:30p—Dinner, lobster appetizers, Dom Perignon '63, 20 oz New York Strip Steak

9:00p—A 1789 bAugier Cognac and Cuban Partagas Lusitanias natural wrapped cigar

10:00p—Sex with three women

11:00p—Massage and Jacuzzi

11:45p—Bed (alone)

11:50p—12 second, 4 octave fart, dog leaves the room

11:55p—Giggle yourself to sleep

Subject: Jack & Jill

Jack was going to be married to Jill, so his father sat him down for a Little fireside chat. He says "Jack, let me tell you something. On my wedding night in our honeymoon suite, I took off my pants and handed them to your mother, and said, here—try these on." So, she did and said, "These just don't fit." So I replied, " . . . exactly. I wear the pants in this family and I always will. Ever since that night we have never had any problems." "Hmmm," says Jack. He thinks that might be a good thing to try. So on his honeymoon Jack takes off his pants and says to Jill, "Here try these on." So she does and says, "these just won't work.." So Jack says, " . . . exactly. I wear the pants in this family and I always will, and I don't want you to ever forget that." Then Jill takes off her pants and hands them to Jack and says, "here you try on mine." So he does and says, "I can't get into your pants." So Jill says, "Exactly, And if you don't change your attitude, you never will."

Subject: The Eleventh Husband

A lawyer married a woman who had previously divorced ten husbands.

On their wedding night, she told her new husband, "Please be gentle; I'm still a virgin." "What?" said the puzzled groom. "How can that be if you've been married ten times?"

"Well, husband #1 was a Sales Representative; he kept telling me how great it was going to be. husband #2 was in Software Services; he was never really sure how it was supposed to function, but he said he'd look into it and get back to me. husband #3 was from Field Services; he said everything checked out diagnostically but he just couldn't get the system up. husband #4 was in Telemarketing; even though he knew he had the order, he didn't know when he would be able to deliver. husband #5 was an Engineer; he understood the basic process but wanted three years to research, implement, and design a new state-of-the-art method. husband #6 was from ;the union he thought he knew how, but he wasn't sure whether it was his job. husband #7 was in Marketing; although he had a nice product, he was never sure how to position it. husband #8 was a psychiatrist; all he ever did was talk about it. husband #9 was a gynecologist; all he did was look at it. husband #10 was a stamp collector; all he ever did was . . . God, I miss him!!!!!!!!!!!!

But now that I've married you, I'm really excited!" "Good," said the lawyer, "but, why?" "Duh; you're a lawyer. This time I know I'm gonna get screwed!"

Subject: Re: A Betting Man

Guy is sitting quietly reading his paper when his wife sneaks up behind him and whacks him on the head with a frying pan.

"What was that for?" he says.

"That was for the piece of paper in your pants pocket with the name Marylou written on it," she replies.

"Two weeks ago when I went to the races, Marylou was the name of one of the horses I bet on," he explains.

She looks satisfied, apologizes, and goes off to do work around the house.

Three days later he's again sitting in his chair reading when she nails him with an even bigger frying pan, knocking him out cold.

When he comes to, he says, "What the hell was that for?"

"Your horse phoned."

Subject: Old Men and Beavers

An 80-year-old man is having his annual checkup. The doctor asks him how he's feeling.

"I've never been better," he replies. "I've got an eighteen year old bride who's pregnant with my child! What do you think about that?"

The doctor considers this for a moment, then says, "Well, let me tell you a story. I know a guy who's an avid hunter. He never misses a season. But, one day he's in a bit of a hurry and he accidentally grabs his umbrella instead of his gun. So he's walking in the woods near a creek and suddenly he spots a beaver in some brush in front of him. He raises up his umbrella, points it at the beaver and squeezes the handle. *BAM* The beaver drops dead in front of him."

"That's impossible!" said the old man in disbelief, "Someone else must have shot that beaver."

"Exactly!"

Subject: For the Ladies

Dear wife:

You must realize that you are 54 years old, and I have certain needs which you are no longer able to satisfy. I am otherwise happy with you as a wife, and I sincerely hope you will not be hurt or offended to learn that by the time you receive this letter, I will be at the Grand Hotel with my 18-year old teaching assistant. I will be home before midnight.

Your husband

When he arrived at the hotel, there was a faxed letter waiting for him that read as follows:

Dear husband:

You, too, are 54 years old and by the time you receive this letter, I will be at the Breakwater Hotel with my 18-year old pool boy. Since you are a mathematician, you will appreciate that 18 goes into 54 more times than 54 goes into 18. Therefore, DON'T WAIT UP!!

Your wife

Subject: HEADACHE

The husband emerged from the bathroom naked and was climbing into bed when his wife complained, as usual, "I have a headache."

"Perfect," her husband said. "I was just in the bathroom powdering my dick with aspirin. You can take it orally or as a suppository, it's up to you !!

Subject: The good, the bad, and the ugly

Good: Your hubby and you agree, no more kids Bad: You can't find your birth control pills Ugly: Your daughter borrowed them

Good: Your son studies a lot in his room Bad: You find several porn movies hidden there Ugly: You're in them

Good: Your husband understands fashion Bad: He's a cross dresser Ugly: He looks better than you

Good: Your son's finally maturing Bad: He's involved with the woman next door Ugly: So are you

Good: You give the birds and bees talk to your daughter Bad: She keeps interrupting Ugly: With corrections

Good: Your wife's not talking to you Bad: She wants a divorce Ugly: She's a lawyer

Good: The postman's early Bad: He's wearing fatigues and carrying an AK47 Ugly: You gave him nothing for Christmas.

Subject: A Barbie We Can Relate to

1. Bifocals Barbie. Comes with her own set of blended-lens fashion frames in six wild colors (half-frames too!), neck chain and large-print editions of Vogue and Martha Stewart Living.

2. Hot Flash Barbie. Press Barbie's bellybutton and watch her face turn beet red while tiny drops of perspiration appear on her forehead. Comes with hand-held fan and tiny tissues.

3. Facial Hair Barbie. As Barbie's hormone levels shift, see her whiskers grow. Available with teensy tweezers and magnifying mirror.

4. Flabby Arms Barbie. Hide Barbie's droopy triceps with these new, roomier-sleeved gowns. Good news on the tummy front, too-muumuus with tummy-support panels are included.

5. Bunion Barbie. Years of disco dancing in stiletto heels have definitely taken their toll on Barbie's dainty arched feet. Soothe her sores with the pumice stone and plasters, then slip on soft terry mules.

6. No-More-Wrinkles Barbie. Erase those pesky crow's-feet and lip lines with a tube of Skin Sparkle-Spackle, from Barbie's own line of exclusive age-blasting cosmetics.

7. Soccer Mom Barbie. All that experience as a cheer-leader is really paying off as Barbie dusts off her old high school megaphone to root for Babs and Ken, Jr. Comes with minivan in robin-egg blue or white, and cooler filled with doughnut holes and fruit punch.

8. Mid-life Crisis Barbie. It's time to ditch Ken. Barbie needs a change, and Alonzo (her personal trainer) is just what the doctor ordered, along with Prozac. They're hopping in her new red Miata and heading for the Napa Valley to open a B&B. Includes a real tape of "Breaking Up Is Hard to Do."

9. Divorced Barbie. Sells for $199.99. Comes with Ken's house, Ken's car, and Ken's boat.

10. Recovery Barbie. Too many parties have finally caught up with the ultimate party girl. Now she does Twelve Steps instead of dance steps. Clean and sober, she's going to meetings religiously. Comes with a little copy of The Big Book and a six-pack of Diet Coke.

11. Post-Menopausal Barbie. This Barbie wets her pants when she sneezes, forgets where she puts things, and cries a lot. She is sick and tired of Ken sitting on the couch watching the tube, clicking through the channels. Comes with Depends and Kleenex. As a bonus this year, the book "Getting In Touch with Your Inner Self" is included.

Subject: Overly Organized

An elderly man lay dying in his bed. In death's agony, he suddenly smells the aroma of his favorite chocolate chip cookies wafting up the stairs. He gathers his remaining strength and lifts himself from his bed. Leaning against the wall, he slowly makes his way out of the bedroom and down the stairs, gripping the railing with both frail hands. Finally, he comes to the doorframe, gazing into the kitchen.

Were it not for death's agony, he would have thought himself already in heaven: there, spread out on the kitchen table were literally hundreds of his favorite chocolate chip cookies. Was he in heaven? Could this possible be one final act of love from his devoted wife?

Mustering one great final effort, he threw himself toward the table, landing on his knees in a rumpled posture. The ancient, withered hand trembled toward a cookie at the edge of the table when it was suddenly smacked with a spatula by his wife.

"Stay out of those," she said, "they're for the funeral."

Subject: A Slip of the Tongue

Two gentlemen with back eyes sit next to one another on a plane bound for Pittsburgh.

"How did you get yours," one asks.

The other replies, " I was at the ticket counter and a beautiful girl with massive breasts waited on me. I said I'd like a picket to Tittsburgh and she hit me. Just a little slip of the tongue."

The first guy says, " Mine was a tongue twister too. I was at the breakfast table with my wife and I wanted to say 'Please pass the Grape Nuts, honey" but I accidentally said "You have ruined my life you evil, self-centered, fat-assed bitch.'"

Subject: What if Dear Abbey was a Man

Dear Abner:
My boyfriend still has feelings for his old girlfriends. I'm afraid he will not be faithful. "Worried"
Dear Worried:
A man's capacity for love is boundless. It has been proven to increase with the number of sexual partners. Thus, by having a few other women, your partner is really increasing his love for you. Best thing to do is to buy your boyfriend a nice bass boat, cook him a nice meal and don't mention this aspect of his behavior.

Dear Abner:
My boyfriend has too many nights out with "the boys". "Alone"
Dear Alone:
This is perfectly natural behavior and should be encouraged. Man is a hunter and needs to prove his prowess with other men. Far from being pleasurable, a night out is stressful and to get back to you is a relief. Best thing to do is to buy him a new hunting rifle and cook him a good meal.

Dear Abner:
My husband wants to experience a menage a trois with me and my sister. What should I do? "Monogamous"
Dear Monogamous:
Your husband is clearly devoted to you. He cannot get

enough of you, so he goes for the next best thing: your sister. Far from being an issue, this will bring the whole family together. Why not get some cousins involved? If you are still apprehensive, then let him go with your relatives. Buy him a Rolex and cook him a nice meal.

Dear Abner:
My husband has never given me an orgasm. " Frustrated"
Dear Frustrated:
The female orgasm is a myth. It is fostered by militant, man-hating feminists and is a danger to the family unit. Don't ever mention it to your husband and show your love by getting him a Harley-Davidson Sportster. Don't forget to cook him a delicious meal.

Subject: It's a Brand New World

Once upon a time, in a land far away, a beautiful, independent, self-assured princess happened upon a frog as she sat contemplating ecological issues on the shores of an unpolluted pond in a verdant meadow near her castle.

The frog hopped onto the princess' lap and said, "Elegant lady, I was once a handsome prince until an evil witch cast a spell on me. One kiss from you, however, and I will turn back into a dapper, young prince. Then we can marry and set up housekeeping in my castle with my mother, where you can prepare my meals, clean my clothes, bear my children and we will live happily ever after."

That night, on a repast of pan fried frog legs seasoned in a white wine and onion cream sauce, the princess chuckled to herself and thought, "I don't think so."

REALITY

No matter how good she looks right now, somebody, somewhere is tired of putting up with her shit.

```
Soccer Shirt  -    $ 59.00
Shin Gaurds  -    $ 12.99
Soccer Cleats - 89.00
```

```
Exposing your package in
front of 100,000 Fans  -
          PRICELESS
```

Chapter Five

VERY OBJECTIONABLE

Subject: Teen Attire

A young punk gets on the cross-town bus. He's got spiked, multicolored hair that's green, purple & orange. His clothing is a tattered mix of leather rags. His legs are bare and he's without shoes. His entire face and body are riddled with pierced jewelry and his earrings are big, bright red, yellow and green feathers. He sits down in the only vacant seat, directly across from an old man who just glares at him for the next ten miles. Finally the punk gets self-conscious and yells at the old man, "What are you looking at you old fart! Didn't you do anything wild when you were young?" Without missing a beat the old man replied, "Yeah. Back when I was very young and in the Navy, I got really drunk in Singapore and had sex with a parrot. I thought you might be my son."

Subject: His face looks like a glazed doughnut

Cinderella wants to go to the ball, but her wicked stepmother won't let her. As Cinderella sits crying in the garden, her fairy godmother appears, and promises to provide Cinderella with everything she needs to go to the ball, but only on two conditions. "First, you must wear a diaphragm." Cinderella agrees. "What's the second condition?" "You must be home by 2 a.m. Any later, and your diaphragm will turn into a pumpkin." Cinderella agrees to be home by 2 a.m. The appointed hour comes and goes, and Cinderella doesn't show up. Finally, at 5 a.m., Cinderella shows up, looking love-struck and **very** satisfied. "Where have you been?" demands the fairy godmother. "Your diaphragm was supposed to turn into a pumpkin three hours ago!!!" "I met a prince, Fairy Godmother. He took care of everything." "I know of no prince with that kind of power! Tell me his name!" "I can't remember, exactly . . . Peter Peter, something or other…

Subject: Weenies

Two Scottish nuns have just arrived in the USA by boat and one says to the other, "I hear that the people of this country actually eat dogs." "Odd," her companion replies, "but if we shall live in America, we might as well do as the Americans do." Nodding emphatically, the mother superior points to a hot dog vendor and they both walk towards the cart. "Two dogs, please," says one. The vendor is only too pleased to oblige, wraps both hot dogs in foil and hands them over the counter. Excited, the nuns hurry to a bench and begin to unwrap their 'dogs.' The mother superior is first to open hers. She begins to blush and, then, staring at it for a moment, leans to the other nun and whispers cautiously, "What part did you get?"

Subject: Home for Lunch

Watch out when you go home for lunch. An exquisite painting, entitled "Home for Lunch", was on display in a northeast Pennsylvania art gallery. It depicted three very naked
and very black men, sitting on a park bench. What was unusual is that the men on both ends of the bench have black
penises, but the man in the middle has a very pink penis.
Two women were standing there, staring at the painting,
scratching their heads, and trying to figure the painting out.
The artist walked by and noticed the women's confusion.
"Can I help you with this painting?" he asked. "Well, yes" said
the one woman. "We were curious about the picture of the
black men on the bench. Why does the man in the middle
have a pink penis?" "Oh," said the artist. "I'm afraid you've
misinterpreted the painting. The three men are not Afri-
can-Americans. They're Pennsylvania coal miners, and the
fellow in the middle went "Home for Lunch."

Subject: She left at the stoke of midnight

This was in the Washington Post—The title of the article was "Best Comeback Line Ever."

Police arrested Patrick Lawrence, a 22-year-old white male, resident of Dacula, GA, in a pumpkin patch at 11:38 p.m. Friday.

Lawrence will be charged with lewd and lascivious behavior, public indecency, and public intoxication at the Gwinnett County courthouse on Monday.

The suspect allegedly stated that as he was passing a pumpkin patch, he decided to stop. "You know, a pumpkin is soft and squishy inside, and there was no one around here for miles. At least I thought there wasn't, "he stated in a phone interview from the Lawrenceville jail.

Lawrence went on to state that he pulled over to the side of the road, picked out a pumpkin that he felt was appropriate to his purposes, cut a hole in it, and proceeded to satisfy his need."

"I guess I was just really into it, you know?" he commented with evident embarrassment. In the process, Lawrence apparently failed to notice the Gwinnett County police car approaching and was unaware of his audience until Officer Brenda Taylor approached him.

"It was an unusual situation, that's for sure," said Officer Taylor. "I walked up to (Lawrence) and he's . . . just working away at this pumpkin."

Taylor went on to describe what happened when she approached Lawrence. "I just went up and said, "Excuse me sir, but do you realize that you are screwing a pumpkin?"

He got real surprised, as you'd expect, and then looked me straight in the face and said, "A pumpkin? Damn . . . is it midnight already?

Subject: Tricks of the Trade

Koala and the Prostitute
A koala bear was approached by a prostitute. Since he had never been with one before, he was curious and excited. They spent the night together in a hotel, and he went down on her the next morning one last time before departing. As he was heading for the door, the prostitute yelled, "Hey, what about my money?" The koala turned, gave her a puzzled look and shrugged his shoulders. She said, "Come here", and pulled a dictionary out of her purse. She pointed to the word "prostitute" and its definition, "Has sex and gets paid." Finally understanding, the koala borrowed her dictionary, turned to the word "koala" and showed her, "Eats bush and leaves."

Subject: Oh Baby, It's Cold Outside

An Amish woman and her daughter were riding in an old buggy one cold, blustery January day. The daughter said to the mother, "My hands are freezing cold."

The mother replied, "Put your hands between your legs. The body heat will warm them up." So the daughter did, and her hands warmed up.

The next day, the daughter was riding with her boyfriend, and he said, "My hands are freezing cold." The daughter replied, "Put them between my legs, they'll warm up."

The next day, the boyfriend was again driving in the buggy with the Daughter. He said, "My nose is freezing cold." The daughter replied, "Put it between my legs. It will warm up." He did, and his nose warmed up.

The next day, the boyfriend was once again driving with the daughter and he said, "My penis is frozen solid."

The next day, the daughter is driving in the buggy with

her mother, and she says to her mother, "Have you ever heard of a penis?"

The slightly concerned mother says, "Sure, why do you ask?"

The daughter says, "Well, they make one hell of a mess when they defrost!"

Subject: Turnabout is fair play

A successful businessman flew to Vegas for the weekend to gamble. He lost the shirt off his back, and had nothing left but a quarter and the second half of his round trip ticket—If he could just get to the airport he could get himself home. So he went out to the front of the casino where there was a cab waiting. He got in and explained his situation to the cabbie. He promised to send the driver money from home, he offered him his credit card numbers, his drivers license number, his address, etc. but to no avail.

The cabbie said (adopt appropriate dialect), "If you don't have fifteen dollars, get the hell out of my cab!" So the businessman was forced to hitchhike to the airport and was barely in time to catch his flight.

One year later the businessman, having worked long and hard to regain his financial success, returned to Vegas and this time he won big. Feeling pretty good about himself, he went out to the front of the casino to get a cab ride back to the airport. Well, who should he see out there, at the end of a long line of cabs, but his old buddy who had refused to give him a ride when he was down on his luck. The businessman thought for a moment about how he could make the guy pay for his lack of charity, and he hit on a plan.

The businessman got in the first cab in the line, "How much for a ride to the airport," he asked? "Fifteen bucks," came the reply. "And how much for you to go down on me (oral sex) during the way?" "What?! Get Out of my cab, you scum." The businessman got into the back of each cab in the long line and asked the same questions, with the same re-sult—getting kicked out of each taxi.

When he got to his old friend at the back of the line, he got in and asked "How much for a ride to the airport?" The cabbie replied "fifteen bucks." The businessman said "O.K." and off they went. Then, as they drove slowly past the long line of cabs the businessman gave a big smile and thumbs up sign to each driver.

Subject: The Freeway of Love

There was a little boy sitting on the curb in front of his house. In one hand he held a package of M&Ms and in the other a cat. Well, the nosey neighbor across the street noticed him sitting there on the curb, and wondered what he was doing.

Closer observation of the little boy brought shock at the sight. Little Bobby would put an M&M in his mouth, bite the cat on the butt, and then scoot down the curb a little bit.

The neighbor stared with wonder as little Bobby kept doing the same thing over and over again. He would put an M&M in his mouth, then bite the cat on the butt, and pro-ceed to scoot down the curb a little further each time.

The neighbor, now growing more concerned, started to walk towards little Bobby when he did it again. He put an M&M in his mouth, bit the cat on the butt, and scooted fur-ther down the curb.

When the neighbor reached little Bobby he said, "What are you doing there little Bobby?"

Bobby said, with a shrug. "Oh. Just playin Truck Driver."

"Truck Driver?" asked the neighbor in perplexity.

"Yes," Bobby answered quite casually. "I'm poppin' pills, eatin pussy, and movin on down the road."

Subject: kitty

A typical married couple were lying in bed one night. The wife had curled up ready to go to sleep and the husband put his bedlamp on to read a book.

As he was reading, he paused and reached over to his wife and started fondling her "kitty". He did this only for a very short while, then he would stop and resume reading his book.

After a few minutes of more reading, he reached over to his wife and started fondling her "kitty" again. Moments later, he resumed his reading.

The wife gradually became aroused with this, and thought that her husband was seeking some response as encouragement before going any further.

She got up and started stripping in front of him. The husband was confused and asked, "What are you doing taking your clothes off?"

The wife replied, "You were playing with my "kitty". I thought it was foreplay to stimulate making love with you tonight.

The husband said, "No, not at all."

The wife then asked," Well, what the hell were you doing then?"

"I was just wetting my fingers so I could turn the pages in my book!"

Subject: Photographers !!!

The Smiths had tried for years to have a child and not having had any luck, decided to use a proxy father to start their family.

On the day the proxy father was to arrive, Mr. Smith kissed his wife and said, "I'm off. The man should be here soon".

Half an hour later, just by chance, a door-to-door baby photographer rang the doorbell, hoping to make a sale.

"Good morning madam. You don't know me but I've come to . . ."

"Oh, no need to explain. I've been expecting you," Mrs. Smith interrupted.

"Really?" the photographer asked. "Well, good! I've made a specialty of babies."

"That's what my husband and I had hoped. Please come in and have a seat. Just where do we start?" asked Mrs. Smith, blushing.

"Leave everything to me. I usually try two in the bathtub, one on the couch and perhaps a couple on the bed. Sometimes the living room floor is fun too; you can really spread out."

"Bathtub, living room floor? No wonder it didn't work for Harry and me."

"Well, madam, none of us can guarantee a good one every time. But if we try several different positions and I shoot from six or seven angles, I'm sure you'll be pleased with the results."

"I hope we can get this over with quickly," gasped Mrs. Smith.

"Madam, in my line of work, a man must take his time. I'd love to be in and out in five minutes, but you'd be disappointed with that, I'm sure."

"Don't I know !!", Mrs. Smith exclaimed.

The photographer opened his briefcase and pulled out a portfolio of his baby pictures. "This was done on the top of a bus in downtown London."

"Oh my God!!", Mrs. Smith exclaimed, tugging at her handkerchief.

"And these twins turned out exceptionally well when you consider their mother was so difficult to work with."

The photographer handed Mrs. Smith the picture.

"She was difficult?" asked Mrs. Smith.

"Yes, I'm afraid so. I finally had to take her to Hyde Park

to get the job done right. People were crowding around four and five deep, pushing to get a good look."

"Four and five deep?" asked Mrs. Smith, eyes widened in amazement.

"Yes," the photographer said. "And for more than three hours too. The mother was constantly squealing and yelling. I could hardly concentrate. Then darkness approached and I began to rush my shots. Finally, when the squirrels began nibbling on my equipment, I just packed it all in."

Mrs. Smith leaned forward. "You mean they actually chewed on your, ummm . . . equipment?"

"That's right. Well madam, if you're ready, I'll set up my tripod so that we can get to work."

"Tripod??", Mrs. Smith looked extremely worried now.

"Oh yes, I have to use a tripod to rest my Canon on. It's much too big for me to hold while I'm getting ready for action. Madam ? Madam? . . . Good Lord, she's fainted !!!"

Subject: a riddle

At the exact same time, there are two young men on opposite sides of the earth: One is walking a tight rope between two skyscrapers. The other is getting oral sex from a 98 year old woman. They are both thinking to themselves the exact same thing. What are they both thinking? The answer is below, but think about it.

Answer: Don't look down

Subject: An Englishman, a Scotsman, and an Irishman

An Englishman, a Scotsman, and an Irishman are all to give speeches to the Deaf Society. All are keen to make an impression on their audience.

The Englishman goes first and to the surprise of his colleagues starts by rubbing first his chest and then his groin.

When he finishes the Scotsman and Irishman ask him what he was doing.

"Well," he explained "by rubbing my chest I indicated breasts and thus, ladies, and by rubbing my groin I indicated balls and thus, gentlemen. So my speech started—Ladies and Gentlemen."

On his way up to the podium the Scotsman thought to himself I'll go one better than that English bastard and started his speech by making an antler symbol with his fingers above his head before also rubbing his chest and his groin.

When he finished his colleagues asked what he was doing. "Well," he explained "by imitating antlers and then rubbing my chest and groin I was starting my speech by saying— Dear Ladies and Gentlemen."

On his way up to the podium the Irishman thought to himself I'll go one further than those mainland bastards and started his speech by making an antler symbol above his head, rubbing his chest, and then his groin, and then masturbating furiously.

When he finished his colleagues asked him what he was doing. "Well," he explained "by imitating antlers, rubbing my chest, then my groin and then masturbating, I was starting my speech by saying—Dear Ladies and Gentlemen, it gives me great pleasure..."

Subject: Don't mess with Bob

The teacher gave her fifth grade class an assignment: get their parents to tell them a story with a moral at the end of it. The next day the kids came back and one by one began to tell their stories.

Kathy said, "My father's a farmer and we have a lot of egg-laying hens. One time we were taking our eggs to market in a basket on the front seat of the pickup when we hit a bump in the road and all the eggs went flying and broke and made a mess."

"And what's the moral of the story?" asked the teacher.

"Don't put all your eggs in one basket!"

"Very good," said the teacher. "Now, Lucy?"

"Our family are farmers too. But we raise chickens for the meat market. We had a dozen eggs one time, but when they hatched we only got ten live chicks. And the moral to this story is, don't count your chickens until they're hatched."

"That was a fine story Lucy. Johnny do you have a story to share?"

"Yes, ma'am, my daddy told me this story about my Uncle Bob. Uncle Bob was a "U.S. Army Special Forces" officer (Green Beret) in Vietnam and his helicopter got hit and he had to bail out over enemy territory and all he had was a bottle of whiskey, an M-60 Machine gun and a machete. He drank the whiskey on the way down so it wouldn't break and then he landed right in the middle of 100 enemy troops. He killed seventy of them with the machine gun until he ran out of bullets, then he killed twenty more with the machete till the blade broke and then he killed the last ten with his bare hands."

"Good heavens," said the horrified teacher, " What kind of moral did your daddy tell you from that horrible story?"

"Don't fuck with Uncle Bob when he's been drinking

Subject: "Nice Ears"

Bob lived in an apartment building and had to walk down the hall every morning to get his mail. One morning while getting his mail, his new, drop-dead gorgeous neighbor came out of her apartment towards him. As she leaned over to get her mail her robe opened a bit. Bob could hardly believe it, she wasn't wearing a thing under her robe. The woman leaned closer to Bob and said good morning.

This time her robe opened up completely. She purred to Bob that she hadn't had a man in years. He could hardly keep eye contact. She said she heard someone coming and that they should go to her apartment.

They went inside and she let the robe fall to the floor. "What do you think my best feature is?"

Bob stuttered and drooled a bit, and finally said, "Your ears."

"What do you mean my ears? Look at me. I have perfect breasts, a nice tight ass, and legs to die for! What on earth made you say ears?"

"Well," said Bob, "in the hall, you said you heard someone coming? That was me!"

Subject: Speech

This guy owns a horse farm and gets a call from a friend. "I know this midget with a speech impediment who wants to buy a horse and I'm sending him over".

The midget arrives and the owner asks him if he wants a male or female horse.

"A female horth," the midget replies. So the owner shows him one.

"Nith looking horth, can I see her mouf?" So the owner picks up the midget and shows him the horse's teeth.

"Nith mouf, can I see her eyeth?" So the owner picks up the midget and shows him her eyes.

"OK, what about the earsth?" Now the owners is beginning to get a little pissed, but he picks up the midget one more time and shows him her ears.

"OK, finally, I would like to see her twat." With that the owner loses all patience, picks up the midget and shoves his head up the horse's twat, and then pulls him out.

Shaking his wet head, the midget says, "Perhapth I should rephrase that. I would like to thee the horth run."

Subject: Acronyms

Three guys and a gal were sitting at the bar talking about their positions in life.

The first guy says," I'm , a YUPPIE, you know, young, urban, professional."

The second guys says, "I'm a DINK, you know, double income, no kids."

The third guy says, "I'm a BUPPIE, you know, black, urban, professional."

They all turn to the woman and wait for her comments.

She says, "I'm a WIFE, you know, wash, iron, fuck, etc.."

Subject: Men Are Like

—laxatives—They irritate the shit out of you
—bananas—The older they get, the less firm they are.
—vacations—They never seem long enough.
—weather—Nothing can be done to change them
—commercials—You can't believe a word they say
—bonds—They take so long to mature
—mascara—They run at the first sight of emotion
—popcorn—They satisfy you, but only for a little while
—snowstorms—You don't know when they are coming, how
    many inches you'll get or how long it lasts

Subject: The origin of Chapstick

The old cowhand came riding into town on a hot, dusty, dry day. The local sheriff watched from his chair in front of the saloon as the cowboy wearily dismounted and tied his horse to the rail a few feet in front of the sheriff.

"Howdy, stranger."

"Howdy, sheriff."

The cowboy then moved slowly to the back of his horse,

lifted its tail and placed a big kiss where the sun don't shine.
He then headed to the bar.

"Hold on mister."

"What's the matter, Sheriff."

"Did I just see what I thought I saw?"

"Reckon you did, Sheriff. I got some powerful chapped lips."

"And that cures them?"

"Nope, but it keeps me from lickin' em."

Subject: If at first you don't succeed....

A minister gave a talk to the local Lion's Club on sex. When he go home, he felt uncomfortable telling his wife about the topic so he said he had discussed horseback riding with the members.

A few days later, the wife ran into some men at the shopping center who had been at the Lion's Club meeting. They complimented her husband on his handling of the topic.

"Yes, I heard. I was surprised about the subject matter, as he has only tried it twice. The first time he got so sore he could hardly walk and the second time, he fell off.

Subject: Wait until you get older

A little girl asked her Mom if she could walk the dog. Mom said, "No. The dog's in heat."

"What's that mean," asked the child

"Go ask you're father. I think he's in the garage."

The little girl finds her father and asks, "Can I take the dog for a walk? Mom says the dog is in heat and I should ask you."

Dad took a rag, soaked it in gasoline and scrubbed the dog's butt with it. "OK, you can go now."

The little girl left and returned in a few minutes.

Dad said, "Where's the dog."

The little girl said, "She ran out of gas about halfway home but don't worry, another dog is pushing her home."

Subject: The Funeral

A woman was leaving the coffee shop with her morning drink when she noticed a most unusual funeral procession approaching the nearby cemetery.

A long black hearse was followed by a second long black hearse. Behind the second hearse was a solitary women walking a pit bull on a leash. Behind her were 200 women in single file.

The coffee drinker could not contain her curiosity. She approached the women walking the dog and said, "I'm sorry for your loss and hate to disturb you but I've never seen a funeral like this. Whose funeral is it?"

The women replied, "My husband is in the first hearse."

"What happened to him."

"My dog attached him and killed him."

"Oh, I'm so sorry. And the second hearse?"

"My Mother-in Law. She was trying to help my husband."

A poignant and thoughtful moment of silence passed between the two women.

"Could I borrow the dog."

"Get in line."

Subject: Take Me Along if You Love Me

A young woman in New York was so depressed that she decided to end her life by throwing herself into the ocean. She went down to the docks and was about to leap into the frigid waters when a handsome young sailor saw her crying on the edge of the pier.

After a brief discussion, he said, "You have a lot to live for.

I'm off to Europe tomorrow-join me. I'll stow you away on the ship, take care of you and feed you every day."

The girl nodded yes. After all, what did she have to lose. Maybe a fresh start in Europe would give her life new meaning. That night the sailor brought her aboard and hid her in a lifeboat.

From then on, every night he brought her food and they made love until dawn. Three weeks later, during a routine inspection, she was discovered by the captain.

"What are you doing here", he asked.

"I have an arrangement with one of the sailors. He brings me food every night and he screws me till dawn until we get to Europe."

"He sure is screwing you, lady", the Captain said. "This is the Staten Island Ferry."

Subject: Quel Hombre

A Texan buys drinks for all in a bar because his wife has just had a twenty pound baby boy. He is "high-fived" all around and a woman faints due to sympathy pains.

Two weeks later the Texan is back in the bar and the bartender asks how much the baby weights now.

The proud father says," Fifteen pounds."

"Why, what happened" asks the bartender.

The Texas father takes a slow swig from his long-neck Lone Star, wipes his lips on his shirtsleeves, leans toward the bartender and proudly says, "Had him circumcised."

Subject: Anatomical Braille

Two deaf people get married. During the first week of marriage, they find that they are unable to communicate in the bedroom with the light out, since they can't see each other signing or lip read.

After several nights of fumbling around and many misunderstandings, the wife figures out a solution.

"Honey, why don't we agree on some simple signals? For instance, if you want to have sex with me, reach over and squeeze my left breast once. If you don't want to have sex, squeeze my right breasts two times."

The husband thinks this is a great idea .He suggests to his wife if she wants to have sex with him "reach over and pull on my penis one time. If you don't want to have sex, pull on my penis two hundred and fifty times.

Subject: You're on the Right Track

One afternoon a little girl returns home from school and announces to her mother that she knows how babies are conceived.

Amused, her mother asks, "Really, Sweetie, tell me all about it."

The little girl patiently explains, "Mommy and Daddy take off all of their clothes, and Daddy's thing stands up and then Mommy puts it in her mouth and it sort of explodes, and that's where babies come from."

Her Mom shook her head, leaned over to meet her eye and said, "Honey, that's not how you get babies. That's how you get jewelry."

dear Captain
My name is Nicola im 8
years. old, this is my first
flight but im not scared. I
like to watch the clouds go
by. My mum says the crew is
nice. I think your plane is
good. thanks for a nice flight
dont fuck up the landing
LUV Nicola
xx x x

Chapter Six

NOTABLE QUOTES? AND TRUE STORIES?

Subject: History repeats itself

1. Abraham Lincoln was elected to Congress in 1846. John F. Kennedy was elected to Congress in 1946.
2. Abraham Lincoln was elected President in 1860. John F. Kennedy was elected President in 1960.
3. The names Lincoln and Kennedy each contain seven letters. Both were particularly concerned with civil rights. Both wives lost their children while living in the White House.
4. Both Presidents were shot on a Friday. Both Presidents were shot in the head.

5. Lincoln's secretary was named Kennedy. Kennedy's secretary was named Lincoln.

6. Both were assassinated by Southerners. Both were succeeded by Southerners. Both successors were named Johnson.

7. Andrew Johnson, who succeeded Lincoln, was born in 1808. Lyndon Johnson, who succeeded Kennedy, was born in 1908.

8. John Wilkes Booth, who assassinated Lincoln, was born in 1839. Lee Harvey Oswald, who assassinated Kennedy, was born in 1939.

9. Both assassins were known by their three names. Both names are comprised of fifteen letters.

10. Lincoln was shot at the theater named 'Kennedy'. Kennedy was shot in a car called 'Lincoln'.

11. Booth ran from the theater and was caught in a warehouse. Oswald ran from a warehouse and was caught in a theater.

12. Booth and Oswald were assassinated before their trials. And here's the kicker . . . A week before Lincoln was shot, he was in Monroe, Maryland. A week before Kennedy was shot, he was in Marilyn Monroe.

Subject: Live Radio

On the morning show at WBAM FM in Chicago, IL they play a game for prizes, usually vacations and such, called "Mate Match." The DJ's ring someone at work and ask if they are married or in a serious relationship. If yes, then this person is asked 3 very personal questions that vary from couple to couple and asked for their significant others name and work phone number. If the significant other answers correctly then they are winners This particular day it got interesting:

DJ: HEY! This is Edgar on WBAM. Do you know "Mate Match"?

CONTESTANT: (laughing) Yes I do.

DJ: What is your name? First only please.

CONTESTANT: Brian

DJ: Are you married or what Brian?

BRIAN: Yes.

DJ: "Yes"? Does this mean your are married, or what Brian?

BRIAN: (laughing nervously) Yes I am married.

DJ: Thank you Brian. OK, now, what is your wife's name? First only please Brian.

BRIAN: Sara.

DJ: Is Sara at work Brian?

BRIAN: She is gonna kill me.

DJ: Stay with me here Brian! Is she at work?

BRIAN: (laughing) Yes she is.

DJ: All right then, first question: When was the last time you had sex?

BRIAN: She is gonna kill me.

DJ: BRIAN! Stay with me here man.

BRIAN: About 8 O'clock this morning.

DJ: Atta boy.

BRIAN: (laughing sheepishly) Well?

DJ: Number 2: How long did it last? Brian: About 10 minutes.

DJ: Wow! You really want that trip huh? No one would ever have said that if it there weren't a trip at stake.

BRIAN Yeah, it would be really nice.

DJ: OK. Final question: Where was it that you had sex at 8 this morning?

BRIAN: (laughing hard) I ummmmm*.

DJ: This sounds good Brian. Where was it?

BRIAN: Not that it was all that great just that her mom is staying with us for a couple of weeks and she was taking a shower at the time.

DJ: Ooooooh, sneaky boy!

BRIAN: On the kitchen table.

DJ: "Not that great"? That is more adventurous than the last hundred times I have done it. Anyway, (to audience) I will put Brian on hold, get his wife's work number and call her up. You listen to this.

DJ: (to audience) Let's call Sara shall we?

CLERK: Kinko's.

DJ: Hey, is Sara around there somewhere?

CLERK: This is she.

DJ: Sara, this is Edgar with WBAM. I have been speaking with Brian for a couple of hours now* SARA: (laughing) A couple of hours?

DJ: Well, a while anyway. He is also on the line with us. Brian knows not to give away any answers or you lose sooooooooo do you know the rules of "Mate Match"?

SARA: No

DJ: Good.

BRIAN: (laughing)

SARA: (laughing) Brian, what the hell are you up to?

BRIAN: (laughing) Just answer his questions honestly OK?

SARA: Oh, Brian*

DJ: Yeah, yeah, yeah. Sara I will now ask you 3 questions and if you answer exactly what Brian has said then the two of you are off to Orlando, Florida at our expense. This does include tickets to Disney World, Sea World and tickets to see the Orlando Magic play. Get it Sara? SARA! GET IT Orlando Magic, they are on strike Sara. Helloooooo anyone home?!?!

SARA: (laughing hard) YES, yes.

BRIAN: (laughing)

DJ: All right, when did you have sex last Sara?

SARA: Oh God, Brian. This morning before Brian went to work.

DJ: What time?

SARA: About 8 I think. (sound effect) DING DING DING

DJ: Very good. Next question: How long did it last?

SARA: 12 to 15 minutes maybe.

DJ: hhmmmmm Background voice in studio: That's close enough. I am sure she is trying not to harm his manhood.

DJ: Well, we will give you that one. Last question: Where did you do it?

SARA: OH MY GOD, BRIAN! You did not tell them did you?!?!

BRIAN: Just tell him honey.

DJ: What is bothering you so much Sara?

SARA: Well, It's just, just that my mom is vacationing with us and. . . .

DJ: She saw?!?!

SARA: BRIAN?!?!

BRIAN: NO, no I didn't.

DJ: Ease up there sister. Just messin' with your head. Your answer?

SARA: Dear Lord, I cannot believe you told them this.

BRIAN: Come on honey it's for a trip to Florida.

DJ: Let's go Sara we ain't got all day. Where did you do it?

SARA: In the ass. (long pause)

DJ: We will be right back. (advertisements)

DJ: I am sorry for that ladies and gentlemen. This is live radio and these things do happen. Anyway, Brian and Sara are off to lovely Orlando, Florida.

Subject: Some Of Life's Ironies

Next time you think you're having a bad day recall that:
1. The average cost of rehabilitating a seal after the Exxon Valdez oil spill in Alaska was $80,000. At a special ceremony, two of the most expensively saved animals were released back into the wild amid cheers and applause from onlookers. A minute later they were both eaten by a killer whale.

2. A psychology student in New York rented out her spare room to a carpenter in order to nag him constantly and study his reactions. After weeks of needling, he snapped and beat her repeatedly with an ax leaving her mentally retarded.

3. In 1992, Frank Perkins of Los Angeles made an attempt on the world flagpole-sitting record. Suffering from the flu he came down eight hours short of the 400 day record, his sponsor had gone bust, his girlfriend had left him and his phone and electricity had been cut off.

4. A woman came home to find her husband in the kitchen, shaking frantically with what looked like a wire running from his waist towards the electric kettle. Intending to jolt him away from the deadly current she whacked him with a handy plank of wood by the back door, breaking his arm in two places. Till that moment he had been happily listening to his Walkman.

5. Two animal rights protesters were protesting at the cruelty of sending pigs to a slaughterhouse in Bonn. Suddenly the pigs, all two thousand of them, escaped through a broken fence and stampeded, trampling the two hapless protesters to death.

6. And the capper. . . . Iraqi terrorist, Khay Rahnajet, didn't pay enough postage on a letter bomb. It came back with "return to sender" stamped on it. Forgetting it was the bomb, he opened it and was blown to bits.

Subject: Sports Wisdom

- Chicago Cubs outfielder Andre Dawson on being a role model: "I want all the kids to do what I do, to look up to me. I want all the kids to copulate me."
- New Orleans Saint RB George Rogers when asked about the upcoming season: "I want to rush for 1,000 or 1,500 yards, whichever comes first."

- And, upon hearing Joe Jacoby of the 'Skins say "I'd run over my own mother to win the Super Bowl," Matt Millen of the Raiders said, "To win, I'd run over Joe's Mom too."
- Football commentator and former player Joe Theismann, "Nobody in football should be called a genius. A genius is a guy like Norman Einstein."
- Oiler coach Bum Phillips: When asked by Bob Costas why he takes his wife on all the road trips, Phillips responded, "Because she is too damn ugly to kiss good-bye."
- Senior basketball player at the University of Pittsburgh: "I'm going to graduate on time, no matter how long it takes."
- Bill Peterson, a Florida State football coach: "You guys line up, alphabetically by height." And "You guys pair up in groups of three, then line up in a circle."
- Clemson recruit Ray Forsythe, who was ineligible as a freshman because of academic requirements: "I play football. I'm not trying to be a professor. The tests don't seem to make sense to me, measuring your brain on stuff I haven't been through in school."
- Boxing promoter Dan Duva on Mike Tyson hooking up again with promoter Don King: "Why would anyone expect him to come out smarter? He went to prison for three years, not Princeton."
- Stu Grimson, Chicago Blackhawks left wing, explaining why he keeps a color photo of himself above his locker: "That's so when I forget how to spell my name, I can still find my @#%#%@ clothes."
- Shaquille O'Neal on whether he had visited the Parthenon during his visit to Greece: "I can't really remember the names of the clubs that we went to."
- Shaquille O'Neal, on his lack of championships: "I've won at every level, except college and pro."

- Lou Duva, veteran boxing trainer, on the Spartan training regime of heavyweight Andrew Golota: "He's a guy who gets up at six o'clock in the morning regardless of what time it is."
- Pat Williams, Orlando Magic general manager, on his team's 7-27 record: "We can't win at home. We can't win on the road. As general manager, I just can't figure out where else to play."
- Chuck Nevitt, North Carolina State basketball player, explaining to Coach Jim Valvano why he appeared nervous at practice: "My sister's expecting a baby, and I don't know if I'm going to be an uncle or an aunt."
- Tommy Lasorda, Dodger manager, when asked what terms Mexican-born pitching sensation Fernando Valenzuela might settle for in his upcoming contract negotiations: "He wants Texas back."
- Darrell Royal, Texas football coach, asked if the abnormal number of Longhorn injuries that season resulted from poor physical conditioning: "One player was lost because he broke his nose. How do you go about getting a nose in condition for football?"
- Mike McCormack, coach of the hapless Baltimore Colts after the team's co-captain, offensive guard Robert Pratt, pulled a hamstring running onto the field for the coin toss against St. Louis: "I'm going to send the injured reserve players out for the toss next time."
- Steve Spurrier, Florida football coach, telling Gator fans that a fire at Auburn's football dorm had destroyed 20 books: "But the real tragedy was that 15 hadn't been colored yet."
- Jim Finks, New Orleans Saints GM, when asked after a loss what he thought of the refs: "I'm not allowed to comment on lousy officiating."
- Lincoln Kennedy, Oakland Raiders tackle, on his decision not to vote: "I was going to write myself in, but I was afraid I'd get shot."

- Frank Layden, Utah Jazz president, on a former player: "I told him, 'Son, what is it with you? Is it ignorance or apathy?' He said, 'Coach, I don't know and I don't care.'"
- Torrin Polk, University of Houston receiver, on his coach, John Jenkins: "He treats us like men. He lets us wear earrings."
- Shelby Metcalf, basketball coach at Texas A&M, recounting what he told a player who received four F's and one D: "Son, looks to me like you're spending too much time on one subject."

Subject: Something to think about the next time you're having a bad day

California examiner, Fire authorities in California found a corpse in a burnt out section of forest while assessing the damage done by a forest fire. The deceased male was dressed in a full wet suit, complete with a dive tank, flippers, and face mask. A post-mortem examination revealed that the person died not from burns but from massive internal injuries. Dental records provided a positive identification. Investigators then set about determining how a fully clad diver ended up in the middle of a forest fire. It was revealed that, on the day of the fire, the person went for a diving trip off the coast— some 20 miles away from the forest. The firefighters, seeking to control the fire as quickly as possible, called in a fleet of helicopters with very large buckets. The buckets were dropped into the ocean for rapid filling, then flown to the forest fire and emptied. You guessed it. One minute our diver was making like Flipper in the Pacific, the next he was doing the breaststroke in a fire bucket 300 feet in the air. Apparently, he extinguished exactly 5'10" of the fire. Some days it just doesn't pay to get out of bed.

The following was taken from a Florida newspaper: A man was working on his motorcycle on his patio and his wife was in the house in the kitchen. The man was racing the engine on the motorcycle and somehow, the bike slipped into gear. The man, still holding the handlebars, was dragged through a glass patio door and, along with the bike, dumped onto the floor inside the house. The wife, hearing the crash, ran into the dining room, and found her husband lying on the floor, cut and bleeding, the motorcycle lying next to him and immediately summoned an ambulance. Because they lived on a fairly large hill, the wife went down the several flights of long steps to the street to direct the paramedics to her husband. After the ambulance arrived and transported the husband to the hospital, the wife uprighted the motorcycle and pushed it outside. Seeing that gas had spilled on the floor, the wife obtained some paper towels, blotted the gasoline, and threw the towels in the toilet. The husband was treated at the hospital and released to come home. After arriving home, he looked at the shattered patio door and the damage done to his motorcycle. He became despondent, went into the bathroom, sat on the toilet, and smoked a cigarette. After finishing the cigarette, he flipped it between his legs and into the toilet bowl while still seated. The wife, who was in the kitchen, heard a loud explosion and her husband screaming. She ran into the bathroom and found her husband lying on the floor. His trousers had been blown away and he was suffering from burns on the buttocks, the backs of his legs and the groin. The wife again ran to the phone and called for an ambulance. The same ambulance crew was dispatched and the wife met them at the street. The paramedics loaded the husband on the stretcher and began carrying him to the street. While they were going down the stairs to the street accompanied by the wife, some of the paramedics asked her how her husband had burned himself. She told them and the paramedics started laughing so hard, one of them tipped

the stretcher and dumped the husband out. He fell down
the remaining steps and broke his arm. Now THAT is a bad
day. . . .

Subject: Stress

A prayer for the stressed:
   Grant me the serenity to accept the things I cannot
change, the courage to change the things I cannot accept,
and the wisdom to hide the bodies of those people I had to
kill today because they pissed me off. And also help me to be
careful of the toes I step on today as they may be connected to
the ass that I may have to kiss tomorrow. Help me to always
give 100 percent at work . . . 12 percent on Mondays, 23 percent on Tuesdays, 40 percent on Wednesdays, 20 percent on
Thursdays, and 5percent on Fridays. And, help me to remember that when I'm having a really bad day, and it seems
that people are trying to piss me off, that it takes 42 muscles
to frown, and only 4 to extend my middle finger and tell
them to bite me!

Subject: Life in the 1500's

Most people got married in June because they took their
yearly bath in May and were still smelling pretty good by June.
However, they were starting to smell, so brides carried a bouquet of flowers to hide the BO
   Baths equaled a big tub filled with hot water. The man of
the house had the privilege of the nice clean water, then all
the other sons and men, then the women and finally the
children. Last of all the babies. By then the water was so dirty
you could actually lose someone in it. Hence the saying,
"Don't throw the baby out with the bath water". Houses had
thatched roofs. Thick straw, piled high, with no wood underneath. It was the only place for animals to get warm, so all the

pets, dogs, cats and other small animals, mice, rats, bugs lived in the roof. When it rained it became slippery and sometimes the animals would slip and fall off the roof. Hence the saying, "It's raining cats and dogs."

There was nothing to stop things from falling into the house. This posed a real problem in the bedroom where bugs and other droppings could really mess up your nice clean bed. So, they found if they made beds with big posts and hung a sheet over the top, it addressed that problem. Hence, those beautiful big 4 poster beds with canopies. I wonder if this is where we get the saying "Good night and don't let the bed bugs bite".

The floor was dirt. Only the wealthy had something other than dirt, hence the saying "dirt poor." The wealthy had slate floors which would get slippery in the winter when wet. So they spread thresh on the floor to help keep their footing. As the winter wore on they kept adding more thresh until when you opened the door it would all start slipping outside. A piece of wood was placed at the entry way, hence a "threshold".

They cooked in the kitchen in a big kettle that always hung over the fire. Every day they lit the fire and added things to the pot. They mostly ate vegetables and didn't get much meat. They would eat the stew for dinner leaving leftovers in the pot to get cold overnight and then start over the next day. Sometimes the stew had food in it that had been in there for a month. Hence the rhyme: "peas porridge hot, peas porridge cold, peas porridge in the pot nine days old."

Sometimes they could obtain pork and would feel really special when that happened. When company came over, they would bring out some bacon and hang it to show it off. It was a sign of wealth and that a man "could really bring home the bacon." They would cut off a little to share with guests and would all sit around and "chew the fat."

Those with money had plates made of pewter. Food with a high acid content caused some of the lead to leach onto the food. This happened most often with tomatoes, so they stopped eating tomatoes for 400 years.

Most people didn't have pewter plates, but had trenchers—a piece of wood with the middle scooped out like a bowl. Trenchers were never washed and a lot of times worms got into the wood. After eating off wormy trenchers, they would get "trench mouth."

Bread was divided according to status. Workers got the burnt bottom of the loaf, the family got the middle, and guests got the top, or the "upper crust."

Lead cups were used to drink ale or whiskey. The combination would sometimes knock them out for a couple of days. Someone walking along the road would take them for dead and prepare them for burial. They were laid out on the kitchen table for a couple of days and the family would gather around and eat and drink and wait and see if they would wake up. Hence the custom of holding a "wake".

England is old and small, and they started running out of places to bury people. So, they would dig up coffins and would take their bones to a house and re-use the grave. In reopening these coffins, one out of 25 coffins were found to have scratch marks on the inside and they realized they had been burying people alive. So they thought they would tie a string on their wrist and lead it through the coffin and up through the ground and tie it to a bell. Someone would have to sit out in the graveyard all night to listen for the bell. Hence on the "graveyard shift" they would know that someone was "saved by the bell" or he was a "dead ringer".

Subject: quote of the New Millennium

Here's the first quotable quote of the millennium. Monica Lewinsky on CNN's Larry King Live discussing her miraculous Jenny Craig weight-loss:

"I've learned not to put things in my mouth that are bad for me."

Subject: Random Facts

1. It is hard to understand how a cemetery raised its burial cost and blamed it on the cost of living.
2. Just remember . . . if the world didn't suck, we'd all fall off.
3. We are born naked, wet, and hungry. Then things get worse.
4. The 50-50-90 rule: Anytime you have a 50-50 chance of getting something right, there's a 90% probability you'll get it wrong.
5. It is said that if you line up all the cars in the world end to end, someone would be stupid enough to try and pass them.
6. Laughing stock—cattle with a sense of humor.
7. You can't have everything, where would you put it?
8. Latest survey shows that 3 out of 4 people make up 75% of the world's population.
9. If the shoe fits, get another one just like it.
10. Eat right. Stay fit. Die anyway.
11. The things that come to those that wait may be the things left by those who got there first.
12. Give a man a fish and he will eat for a day. Teach a man to fish and he will sit in a boat drinking beer all day.
13. Flashlight: A case for holding dead batteries.
14. Shin: A device for finding furniture in the dark.
15. As long as there are tests, there will be prayer in public schools.
16. When you're swimming in the creek, and an eel bites your cheek, that's a moray!
17. A fine is a tax for doing wrong. A tax is a fine for doing well.

18. It was recently discovered that research causes cancer in rats.
19. The only cure for insomnia is to get more sleep.
20. Everybody lies, but it doesn't matter since nobody listens.
21. I wished the buck stopped here, as I could use a few.
22. I started out with nothing, and I still have most of it.
23. When you go into court you are putting yourself in the hands of 12 people that weren't smart enough to get out of jury duty.
24. Light travels faster than sound. This is why some people appear bright until you hear them speak.

Subject: Will Rogers

1. Don't squat with your spurs on.
2. Good judgment comes from experience, and a lot of that comes from bad judgment.
3. Lettin' the cat outta the bag is a whole lot easier 'n puttin' it back in.
4. If you're riding' ahead of the herd, take a look back every now and then to make sure it's still there.
5. If you get to thinking' you're a person of some influence, try orderin' somebody else's dog around.
6. After eating an entire bull, a mountain lion felt so good he started roaring. He kept it up until a hunter came along and shot him . . . The moral: When you're full of bull, keep your mouth shut.
7. Never kick a cow chip on a hot day.
8. There are two theories to arguing with a woman. Neither one works.
9. If you find yourself in a hole, the first thing to do is stop digging.
10. Never slap a man who's chewing tobacco.
11. It don't take a genius to spot a goat in a flock of sheep.
12. Always drink upstream from the herd.

13. When you give a lesson in meanness to a critter or a person, don't be surprised if they learn their lesson.
14. When you're throwing' your weight around, be ready to have it thrown around by somebody else.
15. The quickest way to double your money is to fold it over and put it back in your pocket.
16. Never miss a good chance to shut up.
17. There are three kinds of men: The ones that learn by reading The few who learn by observation The rest of them have to pee on the electric fence for themselves.

Subject: Sometimes it really does take a rocket scientist

Scientists at NASA have developed a gun built specifically to launch dead chickens at the windshields of airliners, military jets and the space shuttle, all traveling at maximum velocity. The idea is to simulate the frequent incidents of collisions with airborne fowl to test the strength of the windshields. British engineers heard about the gun and were eager to test it on the windshield of their new high-speed trains.

Arrangements were made to borrow the gun. But when the gun was fired, the engineers stood shocked as the chicken hurtled out of the barrel, crashed into the shatter proof shield, smashed it to smithereens, crashed through the control console, snapped the engineer's backrest in two, and embedded itself in the back wall of the cabin. Horrified, the British sent NASA the disastrous results of the experiment, along with the designs of the windshield, and begged the U.S. scientists for suggestions.

NASA's response was just one sentence: Thaw the chicken.

Subject: Some customers can't be helped

This is a true story from the Word Perfect Helpline which was transcribed from a recording monitoring the customer care department. Needless to say the HelpDesk employee was fired; however, he/she is currently suing the WordPerfect organization for "Termination without Cause".

Actual dialogue of a former WordPerfect Customer Support employee (now I know why they record these conversations).

"Ridge Hall computer assistance; may I help you?"

"Yes, well, I'm having trouble with WordPerfect."

"What sort of trouble?"

"Well I was just typing along, and all of a sudden the words went away".

"Went away?"

"They disappeared."

"Hmm. So what does your screen look like now?"

"Nothing."

"Nothing?"

"It's blank; it won't accept anything when I type."

"Are you still in WordPerfect or did you get out?"

"How do I tell?"

"Can you see the C: prompt on the screen?"

"What's a sea-prompt?"

"Never mind. Can you move your cursor around the screen?"

"There isn't any cursor: I told you, it won't accept anything I type".

"Does your monitor have a power indicator?"

"What's a monitor?"

"It's the thing with the screen on it that looks like a TV. Does it have a little light that tells you when it's on?"

"I don't know?"

"Well, then look on the back of the monitor and find where the power cord goes into it. Can you see that?"

"Yes, I think so".

"Great. Follow the cord to the plug, and tell me if it's plugged into the wall."

"Yes it is"

"When you were behind the monitor, did you notice that there were two cables plugged into the back of it, not just one?"

"No."

"Well, there are. I need you to look back there again and find the other cable."

"Okay, here it is"

"Follow it for me, and tell me if it's plugged securely into the back of your computer".

"I can't reach it."

"Uh huh. Well, can you see if it is?"

"No."

"Even if you maybe put your knee on something and lean way over?"

"Oh, it's not because I don't have the right angle—it's because it's dark."

"Dark?"

"Yes the office light is off, and the only light I have is coming in from the window."

"Well, turn on the office light then."

"I can't."

"No? Why not?"

"Because there's a power failure."

"A power. . . . A power failure? Aha, Okay, we've got it licked now. Do you still have the boxes and manuals and packing stuff your computer came in?"

"Well, yes I keep them in the closet."

"Good. Go get them, and unplug your system and pack it up just like it was when you got it. Then take it back to the store you bought it from."

"Really? Is it that bad?"

"Yes, I'm afraid it is."

"Well, all right then, I suppose. What do I tell them?"

"Tell them you're too fucking stupid to own a computer."

Subject: Top Sayings We'd Like To See On Those Office Inspirational Posters

1. Rome did not create a great empire by having meetings, they did it by killing all those who opposed them.
2. If you can stay calm, while all around you is chaos, then you probably haven't completely understood the seriousness of the situation.
3. Doing a job RIGHT the first time gets the job done. Doing the job WRONG fourteen times gives you job security.
4. Eagles may soar, but weasels don't get sucked into jet engines.
5. We put the "k" in "kwality."
6. Artificial Intelligence is no match for Natural Stupidity
7. A person who smiles in the face of adversity probably has a scapegoat.
8. Plagiarism saves time.
9. If at first you don't succeed, try management.
10. Never put off until tomorrow what you can avoid altogether.
11. TEAMWORK . . . means never having to take all the blame yourself.
12. The beatings will continue until morale improves.
13. Never underestimate the power of very stupid people in large groups.
14. We waste time, so you don't have to.
15. Hang in there, retirement is only thirty years away!
16. Go the extra mile. It makes your boss look like an incompetent slacker.
17. A snooze button is a poor substitute for no alarm clock at all.
18. When the going gets tough, the tough take a coffee break.
19. INDECISION is the key to FLEXIBILITY.

Subject: More Dumb Blonde

This is especially for the Marine Marathon Runners. If Al Gore is participating this year, remember not to pass him!!

A true Story . . . If, God forbid, she had killed herself, she'd be a shoe-in for the Darwin Award.

Last summer, down on Lake Isabella, located in the high desert, an hour east of Bakersfield, California, a blonde new to boating was having a problem.

No matter how hard she tried, she just couldn't get her brand new 22-ft. Bayliner to perform. It wouldn't get on a plane at all, and it was very sluggish in almost every maneuver, no matter how much power she applied.

After about an hour of trying to make it go, she putted over to a nearby marina, hoping that they could tell her what was wrong. A thorough topside check revealed everything was in perfect working order. The engine ran fine, the outdrive went up and down, the prop was the correct size and pitch.

So, one of the marina guys jumped in the water to check underneath. He came up choking on water, he was laughing so hard.

Under the boat, still strapped securely in place, was the trailer.

Subject: Politically Correct Ways To Say Someone Is Stupid

1. A few clowns short of a circus.
2. A few fries short of a happy meal.
3. The wheel's spinning, but the hamster's dead.
4. All foam, no beer.
5. The butter has slipped off his pancake.
6. The cheese slid off his cracker.
7. Body by Fisher, brains by Mattel.
8. Warning: Objects in mirror are dumber than they appear.

9. Couldn't pour water out of a boot with instructions on the heel.
10. He fell out of the stupid tree and hit every branch on the way down.
11. As smart as bait.
12. Doesn't have all his dogs on one leash.
13. Her sewing machine's out of thread.
14. One fruit loop shy of a full bowl.
15. Her antenna doesn't pick up all the channels.
16. His belt doesn't go through all the loops.
17. Proof that evolution CAN go in reverse.
18. Receiver is off the hook.
19. Not wired to code.
20. Skylight leaks a little.
21. Her slinky's kinked.
22. Too much yardage between the goal posts.
23. Got a full 6-pack, but lacks the plastic thingy to hold them together.
24. A photographic memory, but the lens cover is on.
25. During evolution his ancestors were in the control group.
26. Gates are down, the lights are flashing, but the train isn't coming.
27. Is so dense, light bends around her.
28. If brains were taxed, he'd get a rebate.
29. Standing close to her, you can hear the ocean.
30. Some drink from the fountain of knowledge, but he just gargled.

Subject: Soap Opera

The following letters are taken from an actual incident between a London hotel and one of its guests. The Hotel ended up submitting the letters to the London Sunday Times!

Dear Maid,

Please do not leave any more of those little bars of soap

in my bathroom since I have brought my own bath-sized Dial.
Please remove the six unopened little bars from the shelf
under the medicine chest and another three in the shower
soap dish. They are in my way.

    Thank you,

    S. Berman

Dear Room 635

    I am not your regular maid. She will be back tomorrow,
Thursday, from her day off. I took the 3 hotel soaps out of the
shower soap dish as you requested. The 6 bars on your shelf
I took out of your way and put on top of your Kleenex dispenser in case you should change your mind. This leaves
only the 3 bars I left today which my instructions from the
management is to leave 3 soaps daily. I hope this is satisfactory.

    Kathy, Relief Maid

Dear Maid,

    I hope you are my regular maid. Apparently Kathy did
not tell you about my note to her concerning the little bars of
soap. When I got back to my room this evening I found you
had added 3 little Camays to the shelf under my medicine
cabinet. I am going to be here in the hotel for two weeks and
have brought my own bath-size Dial so I won't need those 6
little Camays which are on the shelf. They are in my way when
shaving, brushing teeth, etc. Please remove them.

    S. Berman

Dear Mr. Berman,

    My day off was last Wed. so the relief maid left 3 hotel
soaps which we are instructed by the management. I took the
6 soaps which were in your way on the shelf and put them in
the soap dish where your Dial was. I put the Dial in the medicine cabinet for your convenience. I didn't remove the 3

complimentary soaps which are always placed inside the medicine cabinet for all new check-ins and which you did not object to when you checked in last Monday. Please let me know if I can be of further assistance.

Your regular maid, Dotty

Dear Mr. Berman,

The assistant manager, Mr. Kensedder, informed me this morning that you called him last evening and said you were unhappy with your maid service. I have assigned a new girl to your room. I hope you will accept my apologies for any past inconvenience. If you have any future complaints please contact me so I can give it my personal attention. Call extension 1108 between 8AM and 5PM. Thank you.

Elaine Carmen, Housekeeper

Dear Miss Carmen,

It is impossible to contact you by phone since I leave the hotel for business at 7:45 AM and don't get back before 5:30 or 6PM. That's the reason I called Mr. Kensedder last night. You were already off duty. I only asked Mr. Kensedder if he could do anything about those little bars of soap. The new maid you assigned me must have thought I was a new check-in today, since she left another 3 bars of hotel soap in my medicine cabinet along with her regular delivery of 3 bars on the bath-room shelf. In just 5 days here I have accumulated 24 little bars of soap. Why are you doing this to me?

S. Berman

Dear Mr. Berman,

Your maid, Kathy, has been instructed to stop delivering soap to your room and remove the extra soaps. If I can be of further assistance, please call extension 1108 between 8AM and 5PM. Thank you,

Elaine Carmen, Housekeeper

Dear Mr. Kensedder,
My bath-size Dial is missing. Every bar of soap was taken
from my room including my own bath-size Dial. I came in late
last night and had to call the bellhop to bring me 4 little
Cashmere Bouquets.
S. Berman

Dear Mr. Berman,
I have informed our housekeeper, Elaine Carmen, of
your soap problem. I cannot understand why there was no
soap in your room since our maids are instructed to leave 3
bars of soap each time they service a room. The situation will
be rectified immediately. Please accept my apologies for the
inconvenience.
Martin L. Kensedder Assistant Manager

Dear Mrs. Carmen,
Who the hell left 54 little bars of Camay in my room? I
came in last night and found 54 little bars of soap. I don't
want 54 little bars of Camay. I want my one damn bar of bath-
size Dial. Do you realize I have 54 bars of soap in here. All I
want is my bath size Dial. Please give me back my bath-size
Dial.
S. Berman

Dear Mr. Berman,
You complained of too much soap in your room so I had
them removed. Then you complained to Mr. Kensedder that
all your soap was missing so I personally returned them. The
24 Camays which had been taken and the 3 Camays you are
supposed to receive daily. I don't know anything about the 4
Cashmere Bouquets, Obviously your maid, Kathy, did not
know I had returned your soaps so she also brought 24 Camays
plus the 3 daily Camays. I don't know where you got the idea

this hotel issues bath-size Dial. I was able to locate some bath-size Ivory which I left in your room.

Elaine Carmen Housekeeper

Dear Mrs. Carmen,

Just a short note to bring you up-to-date on my latest soap inventory. As of today I possess:

On the shelf under medicine cabinet—18 Camay in 4 stacks of 4 and 1 stack of 2.

On the Kleenex dispenser—11 Camay in 2 stacks of 4 and 1 stack of 3.

On the bedroom dresser—1 stack of 3 Cashmere Bouquet, 1 stack of 4 hotel-size Ivory, and 8 Camay in 2 stacks of 4.

Inside the medicine cabinet—14 Camay in 3 stacks of 4 and 1 stack of 2.

In the shower soap dish—6 Camay, very moist.

On the northeast corner of tub—1 Cashmere Bouquet, slightly used.

On the northwest corner of tub—6 Camays in 2 stacks of 3.

Please ask Kathy when she services my room to make sure the stacks are neatly piled and dusted. Also, please advise her that stacks of more than 4 have a tendency to tip. May I suggest that my bedroom window sill is not in use and will make an excellent spot for future soap deliveries. One more item, I have purchased another bar of bath-sized Dial which I am keeping in the hotel vault in order to avoid further misunderstandings.

Subject: Daddy's rules

Daddy's Ten Rules of Dating

1. If you pull into my driveway and honk you'd better be delivering a package because you're sure not picking anything up.

2. You do not touch my daughter in front of me. You may glance at her, so long as you do not peer at anything below her neck. If you cannot keep your eyes or hands off of my daughter's body, I will remove them.

3. I am aware that it is considered fashionable for boys of your age to wear their trousers so loosely that they appear to be falling off their hips. Please don't take this as an insult, but you and all of your friends are complete idiots. Still, I want to be fair and open minded about this issue, so I propose this compromise: You may come to the door with your underwear showing and your pants ten sizes to big, and I will not object. However, in order to ensure that your clothes do not, in fact come off during the course of your date with my daughter, I will take my electric nail gun and fasten your trousers securely in place to your waist.

4. I'm sure you've been told that in today's world, sex without utilizing a "Barrier method" of some kind can kill you. Let me elaborate, when it comes to sex, I am the barrier, and I will kill you.

5. It is usually understood that in order for us to get to know each other, we should talk about sports, politics, and other issues of the day. Please do not do this. The only information I require from you is an indication of when you expect to have my daughter safely back at my house, and the only word I need from you on this subject is: early.

6. I have no doubt you are a popular fellow, with many opportunities to date other girls. This is fine with me as long as it is okay with my daughter. Otherwise, once you have gone out with my little girl, you will continue to date no one but her until she is finished with you. If you make her cry, I will make you cry.

7. As you stand in my front hallway, waiting for my daughter to appear, and more than an hour goes by, do not sigh and fidget. If you want to be on time for the movie, you should not be dating. My daughter is putting on her makeup, a process than can take longer than painting the Golden Gate Bridge. Instead of just standing there, why don't you do something useful, like changing the oil in my car?

8. The following places are not appropriate for a date with my daughter: Places where there are beds, sofas or anything softer than a wooden stool. Places where there is darkness. Places where there is dancing, holding hands, or happiness. Places where the ambient temperature is warm enough to introduce my daughter to wear shorts, tank tops, midriff T-shirts, or anything other than overalls, a sweater, and a goose down jacket should be avoided.

9. Movies with a strong romantic or sexual theme are also to be avoided; movies which feature chain saws are okay. Hockey games are okay. Old folks homes are better.

10. Do not lie to me. I may appear to be a potbellied, balding, middle-aged, dimwitted has-been. But on issues relating to my daughter, I am the all-knowing, merciless God of your universe. If I ask you where you are going and with whom, you have one chance to tell me the truth, the whole truth and nothing but the truth. I have a shotgun, a shovel, and five acres behind the house. Do not trifle with me.

11. Be afraid, be very afraid. It takes very little for me to mistake the sound of your car in the driveway for a chopper coming in over a rice paddy near Hanoi. When my Agent Orange starts acting up, the voices in my head frequently tell me to clean the guns as I wait for you to bring my daughter home. As soon as you pull into the driveway you should exit the car with both hands in plain sight. Speak the perimeter password, announce in a clear voice that you have brought my daughter home safely and early, then return to your car, there is no need for you to come inside. The camouflaged face at the window is mine.

Subject: FHA

For those of you who have had to deal with governmental agencies, this will : strike a familiar and then satisfying chord. : A New Orleans lawyer sought an FHA loan for a client. He was told the loan would be granted if he could prove satisfactory title to a parcel of property being offered as collateral. The title to the property dated back to 1803, which took the lawyer three months to track down. After sending the information to the FHA, he received the following reply (actual letter) "Upon review of your letter adjoining your client's loan application, we note that the request is supported by an Abstract of Title. While we compliment the able manner in which you have prepared and presented the application, we must point out that you have only cleared title to the proposed collateral proper back to 1803. Before final approval can be accorded, it will be necessary to clear the title back to its origin."

Annoyed, the lawyer responded as follows (actual letter)

"Your letter regarding title in Case No. 189156 has been received. I note that you wish to have title extended further than the 194 years covered by the present application. I was unaware that any educated person in this country, particularly those working in the property area, would not know that Louisiana was purchased by the USA from France in 1803, the year of origin identified in our application. For the edification of uninformed FHA bureaucrats, the title to the land prior to USA ownership was obtained by France, which had acquired it by Right of Conquest from Spain. The land came into possession of Spain by Right of Discovery made in the year 1492 by a sea captain named Christopher Columbus, who had been granted the privilege of seeking a new route to India by the then reigning monarch, Isabella. The good queen, being a pious woman and careful about titles, almost as much as the FHA, took the precaution of securing the blessing of the Pope before she sold her jewels to fund Columbus' expedition. Now the Pope, as I'm sure you know, is the emissary of Jesus Christ, the Son of God. And God, it is commonly accepted, created this world. Therefore, I believe it is safe to presume that He also made that part of the world called Louisiana. He, therefore, would be the owner of origin. I hope you find His original claim to be satisfactory. Now, may we have our loan?"

They got it.

Subject: I Wish I Was in Dixie?

The top 40 things you will never, ever, hear a Southerner say,
No matter how much they had to drink or no matter how far
from the South they are:
40: Oh I just couldn't, hell, she's only sixteen.
39: I'll take Shakespeare for 1000, Alex.
38: Duct tape won't fix that.
37: Honey, I think we should sell the pickup and buy a family
    sedan.
36: Come to think of it, I'll have a Heineken.
35: We don't keep firearms in this house.
34: Has anybody seen the sideburns trimmer?
33: You can't feed that to the dog.
32: I thought Graceland was tacky.
31: No kids in the back of the pickup, it's just not safe.
30: Wrestling's fake.
29: Honey, did you mail that donation to Greenpeace?

28: We're Vegetarians.

27: Do you think my gut is too big?

26: I'll have grapefruit and grapes instead of biscuits and gravy.

25: Honey, we don't need another dog.

24: Who gives a crap who won the Civil War?

23: Give me the small bag of pork rinds, please.

22: Too many deer heads detract from the decor.

21: Spittin is such a nasty habit.

20: I just couldn't find a thing at Walmart today.

19: Trim the fat off the steak.

18: Cappuccino tastes better than expresso.

17: The tires on that truck are too big.

16: I'll have the arugula and radicchio salad.

15: I've got it all on the C drive.

14: Unsweetened tea tastes better.

13: Would you like your fish poached or broiled?

12: My fiancée, Bobbie Jo, is registered at Tiffany's.

11: I've got two cases of Zima for the Super Bowl.

10: Little Debbie snack cakes have too many grams of fat.

09: Checkmate.

08: She's too young to be wearing a bikini.

07: Does the salad bar have bean sprouts.

06: Hey, here's an episode of "Hee Haw" that we haven't seen.

05: I don't have a favorite college team.

04: Be sure to bring my salad dressing on the side.

03: You All.

02: Those shorts ought to be a little longer, darlin'.

AND THE #1 STATEMENT YOU WILL NEVER HEAR FROM A SOUTHERNER:

01: Nope, no more for me. I'm drivin tonight.

Subject: Dallas Cowboys

A lady in Dallas calls 911. Hysterically, she says, someone's just broken into my house, and I think he's going to rape me. The police officer says, I'm sorry, we're really busy at the moment. Just get the guy's jersey number and we'll get back to you.

Q: What do you call 47 people sitting around a TV watching the Super Bowl?

A. The Dallas Cowboys

Q: What's Jerry Jones' biggest concern?

A. Does Bail Money count against the Salary Cap?

Q. What do you call a drug ring in Dallas?

A. A huddle.

Q Four Dallas Cowboys in a car, who's driving?

A. The police.

Q. Why can't Michael Irvin get into a huddle on the field anymore?

A. It is a parole violation for him to associate with known felons.

Q How do the Dallas Cowboys spend their first week at spring training?

A. Studying the Miranda Rights.

Q. What's the difference between a Cowboys fan and a baby?

A. Eventually even the baby stops whining.

Subject: More Dallas Cowboys

1. Doctors say because of Michael Irvin's broken clavicle, it will be 6-8 weeks before he can videotape a teammate having sex.

2. I understand Chicago is trying to sign Michael Irvin. They got rid of the refrigerator, so now they want a coke machine.

3. The Dallas newspapers reported yesterday that Texas Stadium is going to take out artificial turf because the Cowboys play better on grass.
4. The Dallas Cowboys adopted a new Honor System. Yes, your Honor. No, your Honor.
5. The Cowboys had a 12 and 5 season last year. 12 arrests, 5 convictions.
6. The Cowboys knew they had to do something for their defense, so they hired a new defensive coordinator: Johnny Cochran.

Subject: 100 Years ago

- The average life expectancy in the United States was forty-seven.
- Only 14 percent of the homes in the United States had a bathtub.
- Only 8 percent of the homes had a telephone.
- A three-minute call from Denver to New York City cost $11.00.
- There were only 8,000 cars in the US and only 144 miles of paved roads.
- The maximum speed limit in most cities was ten mph.
- Alabama, Mississippi, Iowa, and Tennessee were each more heavily populated than California. With a mere 1.4 million residents California was only the twenty-first most populous state in the Union.
- The tallest structure in the world was the Eiffel Towel.
- The average wage in the US was twenty-two cents an hour.
- The average US worker made between $200 and $400 per year.
- A competent accountant could expect to earn $2000 per year, a dentist, $2500 per year, a veterinarian between $1500 and $4000 per year, and a mechanical engineer about $5000 per year.

- More than 95 percent of all births in the United States took place at home.
- Ninety percent of all US physicians had no college education. Instead, they attended medical schools, many of which were condemned in the press and by the government as substandard.
- Sugar cost four cents a pound. Eggs were fourteen cents a dozen.
- Coffee cost fifteen cents a pound.
- Most women only washed their hair once a month and used borax or egg yolks for shampoo.
- Canada passed a law prohibiting poor people from entering the country for any reason, either as travelers or immigrants.
- The five leading causes of death in the US were: 1. Pneumonia and influenza, 2. Tuberculosis, 3. Diarrhea, 4. Heart disease, 5. Stroke.
- The American flag had 45 stars. Arizona, Oklahoma, New Mexico, Hawaii and Alaska hadn't been admitted to the Union yet.
- Drive-by shootings in which teenage boys galloped down the street on horses and started randomly shooting at houses, carriages, or anything else that caught their fancy were an ongoing problem in Denver and other cities in the West.
- The population of Las Vegas, Nevada was thirty. The remote desert community was inhabited by only a handful of ranchers and their families.
- Plutonium, insulin, and antibiotics hadn't been discovered yet. Scotch tape, crossword puzzles, canned beer, and iced tea hadn't been invented.
- There was no Mother's Day or Father's Day.
- One in ten US adults couldn't read or write.
- Only 6 percent of all Americans had graduated from high school.

- Some medical authorities warned that professional seamstresses were apt to become sexually aroused by the steady rhythm, hour after hour of the sewing machine's foot pedals. They recommended slipping bromide—which was thought to diminish sexual desire—into the women's drinking water.
- Marijuana, heroin, and morphine were all available over the counter at corner drugstores. According to one pharmacist, "Heroin clears the complexion, gives buoyancy to the mind, regulates the stomach and the bowels, and is, in fact, a perfect guardian of health."
- Coca-Cola contained cocaine instead of caffeine.
- Punch-card data processing had recently been developed, and early predecessors of the modern computer were used for the first time by the government to help compile the 1900 census.
- Eighteen percent of households in the United States had at least one full-time servant or domestic.
- There were about 230 reported murders in the US annually.

Subject: OW!!!!

Hi Sue,

Just another note from your bottom dwelling brother. Last week I had a bad day at the office. I know you've been feeling down lately at work, so I thought I would share my dilemma with you to make you realize it's not so bad after all. Before I can tell you what happened to me, I first must bore you with a few technicalities of my job. As you know my office lies at the bottom of the sea. I wear a suit to the office. It's a wetsuit. This time of year the water is quite cool. So what we do to keep warm is this: We have a diesel powered industrial water heater. This $20,000 piece of shit sucks the water out of the sea. It heats it to a delightful temp. It then pumps it down to the diver through a garden hose which is taped to the air hose.

Now this sounds like a damn good plan, and I've used it several times with no complaints. What I do, when I get to the bottom and start working, is I take the hose and stuff it down the back of my neck. This floods my whole suit with warm water. It's like working in a Jacuzzi.

Everything was going well until all of a sudden, my ass started to itch. So, of course, I scratched it. This only made things worse. Within a few seconds my ass started to burn. I pulled the hose out from my back, but the damage was done. In agony I realized what had happened. The hot water machine had sucked up a jellyfish and pumped it into my suit. This is even worse than the poison ivy you once had under a cast. Now I had that hose down my back. I don't have any hair on my back, so the jellyfish couldn't get stuck to my back. My ass crack was not as fortunate. When I scratched what I thought was an itch, I was actually grinding the jellyfish into my ass. I informed the dive supervisor of my dilemma over the communicator. His instructions were unclear due to the fact that he along with 5 other divers were laughing hysterically.

Needless to say I aborted the dive. I was instructed to make three agonizing in-water decompression stops totaling 35 minutes before I could come to the surface for my dry chamber decompression. I got to the surface wearing nothing but my brass helmet. My suit and gear were tied to the bell. When I got on board the medic, with tears of laughter running down his face, handed me a tube of cream and told me to shove it "up my ass" when I get in the chamber. The cream put the fire out, but I couldn't shit for two days because my asshole was swollen shut. I later found out that this could easily have been prevented if the suction hose was placed on the leeward side of the ship.

Anyway, the next time you have a bad day at the office,

think of me. Think about how much worse your day would be if you were to shove a jellyfish up your ass. I hope you have no bad days at the office. But if you do, I hope this will make them more tolerable. Take care, and I hope to hear from you soon.

Love you,

Tom

Subject: Twisted Homilies Deep thoughts(?):

1. They call it PMS because Mad Cow Disease was already taken.
2. A fool and his money can throw one hell of a party.
3. When blondes have more fun, do they know it?
4. What happens if you get scared half to death twice?
5. Am I ambivalent? Well, yes and no.
6. He who dies with the most toys is nonetheless dead.
7. Red meat is not bad for you. Fuzzy green meat is bad for you.
8. If you think there is good in everybody then you obviously haven't met everybody.
9. All power corrupts. Absolute power is kinda neat though.
10. Here I am!!! What are your other two wishes?
11. Taxation WITH representation ain't much fun either.
12. A hangover is the wrath of grapes.
13. Confession is good for the soul but bad for your career.
14. Remember: First you pillage then you burn.
15. To err is human. To forgive is against company policy.
16. Honk if you love peace and quiet.
17. Strip mining prevents forest fires.
18. A picture may be worth a thousand words but it uses up a thousand times more memory!
19. If a thing is worth doing wouldn't it have been done already?

Subject: Before the Computer Age

1. An application was for employment
2. A program was a TV show
3. A cursor used profanity
4. A keyboard was a piano!
5. Memory was something that you lost with age
6. A CD was a bank account
7. And if you had a 3 1/2 inch floppy, you hoped nobody found out!
8. Compress was something you did to garbage, not something you did to a file
9. And if you unzipped anything in public, you'd be in jail for awhile!
10. Log on was adding wood to a fire
11. Hard drive was a long trip on the road
12. A mouse pad was where a mouse lived
13. And a backup happened to your commode!
14. Cut you did with a pocket knife
15. Paste you did with glue
16. A web was a spider's home
17. And a virus was the flu!

I guess I'll stick to my pad and paper and the memory in my head. I hear nobody's been killed in a computer crash

Subject: Restroom Signs

- Friends don't let friends take home ugly men.—
  Women's restroom, Starboard, Dewey Beach, DE
- Remember, it's not, "How high are you?" its "Hi, how are you?"—Rest stop off Route 81, West Virginia
- No matter how good she looks, some other guy is sick and tired of putting up with her shit.—Men's Room, Linda's Bar and Grill, Chapel Hill, North Carolina

- A Woman's Rule of Thumb: If it has tires or testicles, you're going to have trouble with it.—Women's restroom, Dick's Last Resort, Dallas, Texas
- Express Lane: Five beers or less—Sign over one of the urinals, Ed Debevic's, Beverly Hills, CA
- You're too good for him.—Sign over mirror in Women's restroom, Ed Debevics, Beverly Hill, CA
- No wonder you always go home alone.—Sign over mirror in Men's restroom, Ed Debevic's, Beverly Hills, CA
- The best way to a man's heart is to saw his breast plate open.—Women's restroom, Murphy's, Champaign, IL
- If you voted for Clinton in the last election, you can't take a dump here. Your asshole is in Washington.—Men's room Outback Steakhouse, Tacoma, Washington
- Beauty is only a light switch away.—Perkins Library, Duke University, Durham, North Carolina.
- If life is a waste of time, and time is a waste of life, then let's all get wasted together and have the time of our lives.—Armand's Pizza, Washington, D.C.
- Don't trust anything that bleeds for 5 days and doesn't die.—Men's restroom, Murphy's, Champaign, IL
- What are you looking up on the wall for? The joke is in your hands.—Men's restroom, Lynagh's, Lexington, KY

Subject: Can You Remember . . .

1. Blackjack chewing gum
2. Wax Coke-shaped bottles with colored sugar water
3. Candy cigarettes
4. Soda pop machines that dispensed bottles
5. Coffee shops with tableside jukeboxes
6. Home milk delivery in glass bottles with cardboard stoppers
7. Party lines

8. Newsreels before the movie

9. P.F. Flyers

10. Butch wax

11. Telephone numbers with a word prefix (like Olive _ 6933)

12. Peashooters

13. Howdy Doody

14. 45 RPM records

15. S&H Green Stamps

16. Hi-fi's

17. Metal ice trays with levers

18. Mimeograph paper

19. Blue flashbulbs

20. Beanie and Cecil

21. Roller skate keys

22. Cork popguns

23. Drive-ins

24. Studebakers

25. Wash tub wringers

If you remembered 0-5 = You're still young If you remembered 6-10 = You are getting older If you remembered
11-15 = Don't tell your age If you remembered 16-25 = You're
older than dirt!

Subject: The right answer

A defense attorney was cross-examining a police officer during a felony trial. It went like this:

Q. Officer, did you see my client fleeing the scene? A. No sir,
but I subsequently observed a person matching the description of the offender running several blocks away.

Q. Officer, who provided this description? A. The officer
who responded to the scene.

Q. A fellow officer provided the description of this so-called
offender. Do you trust your fellow officers? A. Yes sir, with
my life.

Q. With your life? Let me ask you this then officer—do you have a locker room in the police station—a room where you change your clothes in preparation for you daily duties? A. Yes sir, we do.

Q. And do you have a locker in that room? A. Yes sir, I do.

Q. And do you have a lock on your locker? A. Yes sir.

Q. Now why is it, officer, if you trust your fellow officers with your life, that you find it necessary to lock your locker in a room you share with those same officers? A. You see sir, we share the building with a court complex, and sometimes lawyers have been known to walk through that room.

With that, the courtroom erupted in laughter, and a prompt recess was called.

Subject: Advice to Anyone Moving To Texas

1. Save all manner of bacon grease. You will be instructed later on how to use it.
2. Just because YOU can drive on snow and ice does not mean WE can. Stay home the two days of the year it snows. If you do run your car into a ditch, don't panic. Four men in the cab of a four-wheel drive with a 12-pack of beer and a tow chain will be along shortly. DON'T try to help them. Just stay out of their way. This is what they live for.
3. Don't be surprised to find movie rentals and fish bait in the same store.
4. Remember: "Ya'll" is singular "All Y'all" is plural "All Y'all's" is plural possessive.
5. Get used to hearing, "You ain't from 'round here, are ya?"
6. If you are yelling at the person driving 15 mph in a 55 mph zone, directly in the middle of the road, remember: A lot of folks learned to drive on a vehicle known as John Deere, and this is the proper speed and lane position for that vehicle.

7. If you hear a redneck exclaim, "Hey, Y'all, Watch This?" Stay out of his way. These are likely the last words he will ever say.

8. Get used to the phrase, "It's not the heat, it's the humidity." And the collateral phrase "You call this Hot? Wait'll August"

9. There are no Delis. Don't ask.

10. In conversation, never put your hand on a man's shoulder when making a point, especially in a bar.

11. Chili does NOT have beans in it.

12. Brisket is not "cooked" in an oven.

13. Don't tell us how you did it up there. Nobody cares.

14. If you think it's too hot, don't worry. It'll cool down—in December.

15. We do TOO have 4 seasons: December, January, February, and Summer.

16. A Mercedes-Benz is not a status symbol here. A Ford F-350 is.

17. If someone tells you "Don't worry, those peppers ain't hot" you can be certain they are.

18. If you fail to heed my warning in #17 above, be sure to have a bowl of guacamole handy. Water won't do it.

19. Rocky Mountain Oysters are neither from the Mountains nor oysters. Don't ask.

20. If someone says they're "fixin'" to do something, that doesn't mean anything's broken.

21. If you don't understand our passion for college and high school football, just keep your mouth shut.

22. The value of a parking space is not determined by the distance to the door, but the availability of shade.

23. If you see a faster moving vehicle on a two-lane road behind you, pull onto the shoulder. That is what is called "courtesy".

24. BBQ is a food group. It does NOT mean grilling burgers and hot dogs outdoors.

25. No matter what you've seen on TV, Line Dancing is not a popular weekend pastime.
26. Everything goes better with Ranch Dressing or Hot Sauce.

Subject: Martha Stewart's tips for rednecks

General

1-Never take a beer to a job interview
2-Always identify people in your yard before shooting them.
3-It is considered tacky to take a cooler to church
4-If you have to vacuum the bed, consider changing the sheets.
5-Even if you are positive you are in the will, don't drive the u-haul to the funeral

Dining out

1-When decanting wine from the box, tilt the paper cup and poor slowly.
2-If drinking directly from the bottle, hold it in your hands.

Entertaining in your home

1-A centerpiece for the table should not be prepared by the taxidermist.
2-Do not allow the dog to eat at the table, even if his manners are better than cousin Bubba.

Personal Hygiene

1-Ears should be cleaned in private using one's own truck keys.
2-Deodorant is not a waste of good money.
3-Use of toiletries can only delay bathing for a few days.
4-Dirt and grease under nails detracts from jewelry and alters the taste of food.

Dating (Outside the Family)
1-Always offer to bait your date's hook.

Theater Etiquette
1-Refrain from talking to characters on the screen.

Weddings
1-French kissing the bride is dangerous.
2-Livestock is a poor choice for a wedding gift

Driving Etiquette
1-Never tow another car using panty hose and duct tape.
2-When sending your wife down the road with the gas can, do not ask her to bring back beer.
3-At a four way stop, the vehicle with the largest tires does not have right away.

Subject: The real meaning of abbreviations in personal ads.

Women:
40ish—49
Adventurer—Has had more partners than you ever will
Athletic—flat-chested
Average—ugly
Beautiful—average
Contagious Smile—Bring Penicillin
Emotionally secure—medicated
Free spirit—Substance abuser
Fun—Annoying
Good listener—borderline autistic
Old-fashioned—lights out, missionary position only
Outgoing—Loud
Romantic—looks better in candlelight after wine
Widow—nagged first husband to death

Men:

40ish—52 looking for 25 year old

Athletic—watches ESPN

Average—Unusual hair growth on ears, nose and back

Free Spirit—Will sleep with your sister

Fun—Good with a remote and a six pack

Huggable—Overweight, more body hair than a bear

Likes to Cuddle—Insecure mess

Spiritual—Went to church once with his grandmother

Stable—Stalker but never arrested

Thoughtful—Says please when demanding beer

Subject: Job Application

This is an actual job application from a 17 year old boy who submitted it to a McDonald's in Florida. You'll be glad to know they hired him.

Name: Greg Bulmash

Sex: Not yet. Waiting for the right person

Desired Position: President or V.P. Seriously, whatever is available. If I was picky, I wouldn't apply here.

Desired Salary: $185,000 per year plus stock options and a severance package or make an offer.

Education: Yes

Last Position Held: Target for middle management hostility

Salary: Less than I was worth

Reason for Leaving: It sucked

Hours Available: Any

Preferred Hours: 1:30p.m.-2:30p.m. Tuesday and Thursday.

Special Skills: In an intimate environment, yes

May We Contact Your Current Employer: If I had one, would I be applying here?

Can You Lift Up To 50 Pounds?: Of what?

Do You Have A Car: A better question would be "Do you have a car that runs."

Special Awards?: Possible Publishers Clearing House Sweepstakes winner

Do You Smoke?: On the job, no. On break, yes.

What Would You Like To Be Doing In Five Years: Living in the Bahamas with a very wealthy, sexy blonde. I'd like that right now, actually.

Is The Above True And Complete?: Yes. Absolutely

Sign Here: Aries

Subject: Actual Label Instructions on Consumer Goods

Sears Hairdryer: "Do not use while sleeping."

Swanson Frozen Dinners: "Serving Suggestion. Defrost."

Marks and Spencer Bread Pudding: "Product will be hot after heating."

Nytol Sleep Aid: "Warning: May cause drowsiness."

Sainsbury"s Peanuts: "Contains Peanuts."

Swedish Chainsaw: "Do not attempt to stop chain with your hands or genitals."

Subject: Unusual Behavior among Job Applicants

"She wore a Walkman and said she could listen to me and the music at the same time."

"A balding candidate abruptly excused himself and returned wearing a hairpiece."

Interrupted to phone his therapist for advice on answering a specific interview question."

" Said he wasn't interested in the position because it paid to much."

"His briefcase opened when he picked it up and the contents spilled out, revealing ladies panties, perfume and make up."

"Pointing to a black case he carried into my office, he said if he didn't get the job, the bomb would go off. Disbelieving, I told him why he would never be hired and that I was calling the police. He reached down to the case, flipped a switch and ran. No one was injured, but I did need to get a new desk."

Subject: Actual Court Transcripts

Q: What gear were you in at the moment of impact?
A: Gucci Sweats and Reeboks.

Q: What was the first thing your husband said to you when he awoke that morning?
A: He Said, "Where am I, Cathy."
Q: And why did that upset you?
A: My name is Susan.

Q: Now Doctor, isn't it true that when a person dies in his sleep, he doesn't know about it until the next morning.

Q: Were you present when your picture was taken?

Q: So the date of conception of the baby was August 8th?
A: Yes

Q: And what were you doing at the time?

Q: How was your first marriage terminated?
A: By death.
Q: And by whose death was it terminated?

Q: Can you describe the individual?
A: He was about medium height and had a beard.
Q: Was this a male, or a female?

Q: Doctor, how many autopsies have you performed on dead
    people?
A: All my autopsies are performed on dead people.

Q: All your responses must be oral. What school did you go to?
A: Oral.

Q: Doctor, before you performed the autopsy, did you check
    for a pulse?
A: No
Q: Did you check for blood pressure?
A: No
Q: Did you check for breathing?
A: No
Q: So, it is possible that the patient was still alive when you
    began the autopsy?
A: No
Q: How can you be so sure, Doctor?
A: Because his brain was sitting on my desk in a jar
Q: But could the patient have been alive nevertheless
A: Yes, it is possible that he could have been alive and practic-
    ing law somewhere.

Chapter Seven

THE CLINTON LEGACY

Subject: Americans love to help

A Marine colonel on his way home from work at the Pentagon came to a dead halt in traffic and thought to himself, " Wow, this traffic seems worse than usual. Nothing's even moving. "He notices a police officer walking back and forth between the lines of cars so he rolls down his window and asks, "Officer, what's the hold up?" The officer replies, "The President is just so depressed about the thought of moving with Hillary to New York that he stopped his motorcade in the middle of the Beltway and he's threatening to douse himself in gasoline and set himself on fire. He says his family hates him and he doesn't have the money to pay for the new house." I'm walking around taking up a collection for him. "Oh really? How much have you collected so far?" "So far about three hundred gallons but a lot folks are still siphoning!"

Subject: Take me out to the Ballgame

—The President and Mrs. Clinton are in the front row at a Yankees game. The row behind them is taken up with Secret Service agents. One of them leans over and whispers in the President's ear. Mr. Clinton pauses, then grabs Hillary by the scruff of the neck and heaves her over the railing. She falls 10 feet to the top of the dug out, kicking and screaming obscenities. The President shakes hands of those near him and gets high five's'. The Secret Service agent leans over again and whispers, "Mr. President, I said, they want you to throw out the first PITCH."

Subject: Very Shrewd Bargain

President Clinton arrives in DC after a trip to his home state of Arkansas. He steps out of the he plane carrying two pigs, one under each arm. When he reaches the bottom of the stairs, the Marine guard salutes him sharply. Clinton smiles and says, "I'd like to salute back, son, but as you can see, my hands are full." "Yes, sir!" says the Marine. "Mighty fine pigs, sir!" Clinton replies, "These aren't just ordinary pigs, sons; they're pure Arkansas razorbacks." "Yes, sir!" says the Marine. "Mighty fine razorbacks, sir!" Clinton says, "I got one for Hillary and one for Chelsea." "Yes, sir!" the Marine says again. "Good trade, sir!"

Subject: MORE POLITICS

Chrysler Corporation is adding a new car to its line to honor Bill Clinton. The Dodge Drafter will begin production in Canada this year.

When Clinton was asked what he thought about foreign affairs, he replied, "I don't know, I never had one."

Clinton's mother prayed fervently that Bill would grow up and become President of the United States. So far, half of her prayer has been answered.

American Indians have nicknamed Bill Clinton as "Walking Eagle" because he is so full of ___ he can't fly.

Isn't putting Bill Clinton in charge of a trust fund (Social Security) as insane as putting a draft dodger as Commander-In-Chief?

Clinton is doing the work of 3 men: Larry, Curly, and Moe.

Revised judicial oath: "I solemnly swear to tell the truth as I know it, the whole truth as I believe it to be, and nothing but what I think you need to know."

Politicians and diapers have one thing in common. They should both be changed regularly, and for the same reason.

Subject: What happened to spin the bottle

A little boy & a little girl were sitting on the porch. She asks, "Do you wanna get undressed and play doctor?" He replies, "That's too old fashioned. Spit out your gum. I wanna play President."

Subject: More Hillary and Bill

During a recent publicity outing, Hillary took off to visit a fortune teller of some local repute. In a dark and hazy room, peering into a crystal ball, the mystic delivered grave news. "There's no easy way to say this, so I'll just be blunt: Prepare yourself to be a widow. Your husband will die a violent and horrible death this year." Visibly shaken, Hillary stared at the woman's lined face, then at the single flickering candle, then down at her hands. She took a few deep breaths to compose herself. She simply had to know. She met the fortuneteller's gaze, steadied her voice, and asked her question. "Will I be acquitted?"

Subject: Bumper sticker

"Run Hillary Run!" bumper stickers are selling like hotcakes in New York. Democrats put them on their rear bumpers Republicans put them on the front.

Subject: Hillary in Heaven

The Clintons were in a terrible plane crash and all three died. When they got into heaven, they approached the Throne of God and God said to Chelsea, "Why should I let you in heaven?" Chelsea answered, "I am the daughter of the President, a representative of all the children in America."

"Very well, you may sit on my right side." Then God said to Bill," Why should I let you in heaven?" Bill answered, "I am the President of the United States, a representative of all the people in America." God said, "Very well, you may sit on my left side." Then he said to Hillary, "Why should I let you in heaven?" Hillary answered, "I don't know, but you're in my seat!"

Subject: Procrastination

Why is Bill Clinton so reluctant to decide the fate of ElianGonzalez?

Because last time he made a decision about where to put a Cuban, he was impeached.

Subject: Worst Golf Foursome

The worst foursome in golf: 1. MONICA LEWINSKI 2. O.J. SIMPSON 3. TED KENNEDY 4. BILL CLINTON. Why, you ask?? Lewinski is a hooker, O.J. is a slicer, Kennedy can't drive over water, and Clinton can't remember which hole he played last.

Subject: Monica's book titles

Possible titles for Monica Lewinsky's new book: "I Suck At My Job" "What Really Goes Down In The White House" "How I Blew It In Washington" "You Have to Work Hard to Find the Softer Side of the President" "Testing the Limits of the Gag Rule" "Going Back for Gore" "Podium Girl" "I Got Your Secret Service, Right Here!" "Harass is Not Two Words: The Story of Bill Clinton" "Deep Inside The Oval Office" "The Congressional Study on White House Intern Positions" "She's Chief of MY Staff!" "Al Gore Is In Command For The Next 30 Minutes" "How To Beat Off the Government" "Going Down and Moving Up" "Members of the Presidential Cabinet" "Me and My Big Mouth" "How To Get Ahead in Politics"

Subject: He's everywhere

: A woman always wanted an expensive car-a status symbol to drive around and be seen in. She scrimps and saves, goes to the BMW dealer, and plops down several years income for a brand new, state-of-the-art, computer-enhanced, dream mobile.

She's driving off and decides she wants some music and searches for the radio. The dashboard looks like a control panel at NASA. She fiddles with this button and that gizmo, jiggling these and those, but finally gives up. She can't find the darned thing.

Furious, she races back to the dealership and screams at the salesman and tells him they forgot to install the radio.

He assures her it's right there in front of her and that it's hooked into the onboard computer. All she has to do is tell it what she wants. He demonstrates: "Classical," he says. Click The car fills with the sounds of Paganini.

"Blues," she says, and Click a B.B. King classic plays.

She drives off amazed. "Country," she says, and Click a Garth Brooks tune comes on.

"Folk" Click Joan Baez sings about the night they drove ol' Dixie down.

"New Age" Click Yanni at the Acropolis snaps on.

She's so captivated by this new toy that she isn't paying much attention to the road. Another driver runs a light and cuts her off.

"Asshole!" she screams. Click "Ladies and gentlemen, the President of the United States."

Subject: 11th Commandment

Last week a very important meeting took place among God, the Pope and Moses. They were troubled because the President of the United States was behaving in an inappropriate manner.

They decided that the only course of action left was to create an 11th Commandment to get their message across.

Now the problem remained exactly how to word this new commandment so that it matched the other commandments in style & holy inspiration.

After great meditation & discussion, they concluded: "Thou shalt not comfort thy rod with thy staff."

Subject: He's everywhere-Two

A man takes the day off work and decides to go out golfing. He is on the second hole when he notices a frog sitting next to the green. He thinks nothing of it and is about to shoot when he hears, "Ribbit 9 Iron." The man looks around and doesn't see anyone. Again, he hears, "Ribbit 9 Iron." He looks at the frog and decides to prove the frog wrong, puts the club away, and grabs a 9 iron. Boom! He hits it 10 inches from the cup. He is shocked. He says to the frog, "Wow that's amazing. You must be a lucky frog, eh? The frog reply's, "Ribbit Lucky frog." The man decides to take the frog with him to the next hole. "What do you think frog?," the man asks. "Ribbit 3 wood." The guy takes out a 3 wood and, Boom! Hole in one. The man is befuddled and doesn't know what to say. By the end of the day, the man golfed the best game of golf in his life and asks the frog, "OK where to next?" The frog replies, "Ribbit Las Vegas." They go to Las Vegas and the guy says, "OK frog, now what?" The frog says, "Ribbit Roulette." Upon approaching the roulette table, the man asks, "What do you think I should bet?" The frog replies, "Ribbit = $3000, black 6." Now, this is a million-to-one shot to win, but after the golf game, the man figures what the heck. Boom! Tons of cash comes sliding back across the table. The man takes his winnings and buys the best room in the hotel. He sits the frog down and says, "Frog, I don't know how to repay you. You've won me all this money and I am forever grateful". The frog replies, "Ribbit Kiss Me." He figures why not, since after all the frog did for him, he deserves it. With a kiss, the frog turns into a gorgeous 15 year old girl.

"And that, your honor, is how the girl ended up in my room. So help me God or my name is not William Jefferson Clinton."

Subject: Need Instant Replay

WASHINGTON, DC—On the heels of last week's decision to allow witness testimony in the presidential impeachment trial, key witness Monica Lewinsky was subpoenaed Monday to reblow President Clinton on the Senate floor.

The controversial fellatio, which, under the terms of the court order, will involve the full participation of both Lewinsky and the president, was described by Senate leaders as a "regrettable but unfortunately very necessary" move.

"This trial is not about sex, it's about perjury," Senate Majority Leader Trent Lott (R-MS) said. "Our job is to determine whether or not the president lied under oath. Although the Starr Report contained many detailed descriptions, until we see for ourselves, with our own eyes, exactly what took place during these secret rendezvous between the president and Miss Lewinsky, we won't have all the facts necessary to determine if the president's statements before the grand jury constituted a crime."

In addition to fellatio, Lewinsky and Clinton will be required to reenact several other key sex acts in which the pair allegedly engaged, including but not limited to: deep or "French" kissing, under-the-sweater fondling, and vaginal penetration with various objects.

Responding to outraged Clinton defense lawyers, who denounced the reenactment as "a blatant attempt on the part of political enemies of this administration to humiliate the president," chief prosecutor Rep. Henry Hyde (R-IL) insisted that it is necessary to ensure a fair trial.

"How can we rule objectively in this case without all the details? Yes, we know that the president inserted a cigar into Miss Lewinsky's vagina, but just how many inches of it did he manage to work all the way up inside there?" Hyde asked. "What were their exact facial expressions at key moments of ecstatic release? To what extent did Miss Lewinsky's ample bosom bounce to and fro as she vigorously bobbed her head up and down? Precisely how much of the president's erect penis was Miss Lewinsky physically able to force deep into the back of her throat? Was there gagging involved? Were the president's balls, at any point in the proceedings, licked? If we do not explore every possible detail of these shocking improprieties, we will never know the answers to these vital questions of national security."

"If President Clinton has any respect for the Constitution and the citizens of this nation," Hyde added, "he will cooperate fully in these proceedings and allow himself to be sucked off with calm, reserved dignity, without resorting to partisan name-calling. Nothing less than the very future of our country is at stake."

More controversy is expected Friday, when Senate debate is scheduled to begin on the issue of whether the crucial cock suckings will be televised. Though Clinton defense lawyers are fighting to have the reenactments performed in a closed-door session, most senators are demanding that they be included in the regular televised broadcasts of the trial, citing the imperative of the public's "right to know."

"If, as the president says, he is innocent of perjury, with nothing to hide, he should have no reason to fear providing full disclosure—including full frontal nudity, if necessary—before the American people," Sen. Phil Gramm (R-TX) said. "As elected officials, we have taken a solemn oath to serve the interests of those we represent. If we fail to provide the public with the whole truth—no matter how sordid, depraved, perverse or even vicariously titillating it may be—we have failed in our duty to the people of this nation."

In the event that television cameras are allowed, as is expected, complete coverage of the presidential fellating, as well as related "second-" and "third-base" sex acts, will be aired live on C-SPAN. Highlight footage of particularly critical segments, such as genital/anal contact and ejaculation, will also be broadcast on all the prime-time network newscasts.

Due to the enormous public interest in the scandal, as well as the ease of global dissemination via television and the Internet, footage of the Senate-floor coupling is expected to rank among the most widely seen in history, with near-constant re-airings on cable TV likely to last well beyond the year 2015. Many Americans are expressing alarm over such a prospect.

"How am I supposed to explain to my six-year-old daughter that the president is fucking some girl's mouth on TV?" asked Lorraine Sanders, associate director of the What About The Children? Foundation and a staunch presidential-penis-penetration opponent. "For God's sake, she's only a child. An innocent child!"

"This trial is not the sort of thing our kids should be exposed to," said concerned parent Judith LaFleur, who is leading a campaign to place content-warning labels on federal legislators. "Watching the president get his cock feverishly sucked is for mature, responsible adults only." Despite the public outcry, those legislators who are demanding the reblowings remain adamant that the proceedings be televised uncensored and in their entirety, calling it "a matter of ethics."

"This may be the most important issue ever faced by Congress in its 210-year history," Hyde said. "We are talking about the possible removal of the highest elected official in the land, and that is not the sort of matter that should be trivialized."

Subject: Names for Bill & Hillary's New House

A house is not a home until it's got a name—What should be the official name for Bill & Hillary Clinton's New York abode? There were lots of possibilities, according to the creative audience of The Jayne Carroll Show, a political talk radio program which airs daily in the Portland, Oregon metropolitan area. On Friday, September 10th, Carroll asked her audience to come up with an official name for the Clinton $1.7 million house in Chappaqua, New York. Carroll's call-in contest required the names to be in relative good taste, original, and should capture the essence of one or both of the Clintons. The response was overwhelming!

Some names nominated for the Clinton's new home included:

"Perjurers' Palace", "HillBilly Villa", "The House of Bill's Repute", "Drawers Downs", "Cheatem Estates". "Castle of Contempt", "Sin Simeon", "The House That Terrybought", "The Knee Pad", "The White Trash House", "The Blight House", and "The Panderosa".

"Liars' Lair' was a frequent nominee both on and off the air," according to talk host Carroll. "One of my favorite names was "Bill & Hill's Bribe & Breakfast."

More of the over 100 caller nominated names were:

"The Clinton Compost", "Dogpatch on the Hudson", "Rancho Immoral", "Deceitful Domicile", "Monica's Man's Manor", "The Hen House", "The Out House", "The Big House", "The Love Shack", "Lucifer's Lair", "House of the Rising Son", "The House of Seven Felonies", "Cottage of Contempt", and "Motel Sex".

But the clear, hands-down winner was— "DISGRACELAND"!

Subject: Limericks

The result of a contest in Oxnard, California which required the contestants to use the words Lewinski and Kaczynski. Here are the three winners:

Entry #1 There once was a gal named Lewinski, Who played on a flute like Stravinsky 'Twas "Hail to the Chief" on the flute made of beef That stole the front page from Kaczynski

Entry #2 Said Bill Clinton to young Lewinski, We don't want to leave clues like Kaczynski Since you look such a mess use the hem of your dress, And wipe that stuff off of your chinsky

Entry #3 Lewinski and Clinton have shown What Kaczynski must surely have known That an intern is better than a bomb in a letter Given the choice of how to be blown.

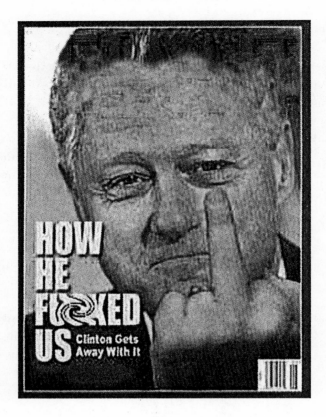

Subject: Anyone can borrow money!

"Hi, Mr. and Mrs. Clinton, welcome to EZBreeZee Mortgages. I'm Allen Greenspan. No, no relation sorry to say. May I call you Bill and Hillary? Fine, first lady Hillary Rodham Clinton and Bill it is.

"So you want to buy the old Rye Brook place, 4-something acres as I recall. That's $2.2 million, and with the customary 20% down, that's $440,000, leaving a mortgage of $1,760,000. No problem. We do those kinds things all the time. Now let's just have a look at your financial statements.

"Let's see. Mr. Clinton, you are the president of the

United States, of course, and your salary is—oh, dear—
$200,000 a year. We recommend buying a house that cost no
more than two and a half times your annual salary. That means
you should be looking for something around $500,000, per-
haps a nice brick rancher on a quarter of an acre not too fancy
a neighborhood?

And I see here that you'll be out of a job in 16 months or
so. What will you do then? Open a library. in Little
Rock,.Arkansas. Wow. I bet that will be some kind of money
maker.

Mrs. Clinton, you're running for Senate, right? Senators
are paid $130,000 a year—assuming of course, she's elected—
so even with your pension you're still looking at a house in
the $825,000 range. Maybe a nice center hall colonial where
the schools aren't so good.

Mrs. Clinton, you haven't worked outside the home since
1991, correct? But you did some volunteer work, I see. You
came up with a plan to overhaul the health care system? I see.
It flopped, in other words.

"But I see you had several business ventures back in Arkansas. How about this Whitewater Development Corp.? It
went bankrupt. And Madison Guaranty? Bankrupt. And Castle
Grande? Bankrupt, too. If you had gone to business school
instead of Yale law, you could probably get your money back.
Don't get upset. It was just a little joke.

"A little bad luck with the law, too, I see. Three of your
business partners went to jail. Maybe you could get your money
back.

"This is an embarrassing question, I know, but we have to
ask because it does, after all, affect your ability to pay: Any
problems with your marriage? No? Fine.

"Let's look at your assets: $1.5 million. Not bad. Yes, yes,
Mr. Clinton, we're not forgetting your Mustang back in Little
Rock. But—those liabilities. You owe $5.5 million. That means
you're $4 million in the hole. How do you expect to pay that

off? You're hoping people will donate to a special fund. So basically you're relying on the charity of strangers.

"You also have some serious expenses. a kid at Stanford has got to be setting you back $30,000 a year, probably more with air fares. And she wants to go to medical school? Ouch!

"And Mr. Clinton. There's a little matter of $90,000 for lying in court. I guess that rules out putting you law degree to work. Say, how do we know your not lying on your loan application? Good point. It would look a lot better if you were lying. Are there any other legal matters we should know about?

"You say you're in the clear, Mr. Clinton, and the first lady is "pretty much in the clear indictment-wise." What does that mean? You don't think—don't think—she's going to get hit with a perjury or obstruction of justice rap. But we're not totally sure, right? That means there's the remote possibility—note that I say "remote" that you could be trying to pay off $1.76 million mortgage while making 12 cents an hour stitching mailbags for the feds and he is trying to make a go of a library in Little Rock.

"Let's review the situation. One of you is now unemployed and the other one soon will be. You have these whopping great debts that you're hoping someone is going to come along and pay. You have a financial history that can only be described as "checkered," plus a bunch of serious financial demands and ongoing legal problems. Your tangible assets seem to consist of an old Ford.

"So CONGRATULATIONS! Welcome to the EZBreeZee family of homeowners! You've got your mortgage!"

This one won't talk, Bill.

Subject: Really applies to both parties

NOTICE FROM THE WHITE HOUSE: PLEASE READ AND
PASS ON TO ALL CONCERNED CITIZENS

Democrats announced today that they are changing their
emblem from a donkey to a condom because it more clearly
reflects their party's political stance. A condom stands up to
inflation, halts production, discourages cooperation, protects

a bunch of dicks, and gives one a sense of security while screwing others.

Subject: Bad Day

It was getting a little crowded in Heaven, so God decided to change the admittance policy. The new law was that, in order to get into Heaven, you had to have a really bummer day on the day that you died. = The policy would go into effect at noon the next day. So, the next day at 12:01, the first person came to the gates of Heaven.

The Angel at the gate, remembering the new policy, promptly asked the man, "Before I let you in, I need you to tell me how your day was going when you died."

"No problem," the man said. "I came home to my 25th floor apartment on my lunch hour and caught my wife having an affair. But her lover was nowhere in sight. I immediately began searching for him. My wife was half-naked and yelling at me as I searched the entire apartment. Just as I was about to give up, I happened to glance out onto the balcony and noticed that there was a man hanging off the edge by his fingertips! The nerve of that guy! Well, I ran out onto the balcony and stomped on his fingers until he fell to the ground. But wouldn't you know it, he landed in some trees and bushes that broke his fall and he didn't die. This ticked me off even more. In a rage, I went back inside to get the first thing I could get my hands on to throw at him. Oddly enough, the first thing I thought of was the refrigerator. I unplugged it, pushed it out onto the balcony, and tipped it over the side. It plummeted 25 stories and crushed him! The excitement of the moment was so great that I had a heart attack and died almost instantly."

The Angel sat back and thought a moment. Technically, the guy did have a bad day. It was a crime of passion. So, the

Angel announces, "OK sir. Welcome to the Kingdom of Heaven," and let him in.

A few seconds later the next guy came up. To the Angel's surprise, it was Vernon Jordan. "Mr. Jordan, before I can let you in, I need to hear about what your day was like when you died."

Jordan said, "No problem. But you're not going to believe this. I was on the balcony of my 26th floor apartment doing my daily exercises. I had been under a lot of pressure so I was really pushing hard to relieve = my stress. I guess I got a little carried away, slipped, and = accidentally fell over the side! Luckily, I was able to catch myself by the finger tips on the balcony below mine. But all of a sudden this crazy man comes running out of his apartment, starts cussing, and stomps on my fingers. Well of course I fell. I hit some trees and bushes at = the bottom which broke my fall so I didn't die right away. As I'm laying there face up on the ground, unable to move and in excruciating pain, I see this guy push his refrigerator, of all things, off the balcony. It falls the 25 floors and lands on top of me killing me instantly."

The Angel is quietly laughing to himself as Jordan finishes his story. "I could get used to this new policy", he thinks to himself. "Very well," the Angel announces. "Welcome to the Kingdom of Heaven," and h lets Vernon enter.

A few seconds later, President Clinton comes up to the gate. The Angel is almost too shocked to speak. Thoughts of assassination and war pour through the Angel's head. Finally he says "Mr. President, please tell me what it was like the day you died."

Clinton says, "OK, picture this. I'm naked inside a refrigerator . . ."

I guess he looks a little like me, but I swear, lady,
I have never seen you before!

Subject: Hillary in Heaven

Hillary Clinton died and went to heaven. St. Peter was giving her a tour when she noticed that there were dozens of clocks on the wall.

Each clock displayed a different time of day. When she asked St. Peter about the clocks, he replied, "We have a clock for each person on earth. Every time they tell a lie the hands move. Their clock ticks off one-second each time a lie is told."

St. Peter pointed out two clocks in particular. "The clock belonging to Mother Teresa has never moved, indicating that she never told a lie. The clock for Abraham Lincoln has only moved twice. He only told two lies in his life."

Hillary asked, "Where is Bill's clock?"

St. Peter replied, "Jesus has it in his office. He's using it as a ceiling fan."

Subject: KFC for Hillary

Kentucky Fried Chicken in New York is offering a special on a "Bucket of Hillary".

Two small breasts, two enormous thighs and a bunch of left wings.

Subject: Hillary's bundle of joy

Given Rudy's recent problems, Hillary decided to go to her Doctor for a physical.

At the end of the exam, the Doctor tells her she is pregnant.

She calls the White House immediately, screaming, "How could you get me pregnant

With all that's going on in my life now!! How could you."

There is nothing but silence on the other end.

She screams again, "HOW COULD YOU!!! CAN YOU HEAR ME???"

Finally she hears Bill's very, very quiet voice. In a barely audible whisper, he says,

"Who is this?"

Subject: Congress Approves Americans With No Abilities Act

WASHINGTON, DC—On Tuesday, Congress approved the Americans With No Abilities Act, sweeping new legislation that provides benefits and protection for more than 135 million talentless Americans. The act, signed into law by President Clinton shortly after its passage, is being hailed as a major victory for the millions upon millions of U.S. citizens who lack any real skills or uses.

"Roughly 50 percent of Americans—through no fault of their own—do not possess the talent necessary to carve out a meaningful role for themselves in society," said Clinton, a longtime ANA supporter.

"Their lives are futile hamster-wheel existences of unrewarding, dead-end busywork: Xeroxing documents written by others, filling out mail-in rebates for Black & Decker toaster ovens, and processing bureaucratic forms that nobody will ever see. Sadly, for these millions of non-abled Americans, the American dream of working hard and moving up through the ranks is simply not a reality."

Under the Americans With No Abilities Act, more than 25 million important-sounding "middle man" positions will be created in the white-collar sector for non-abled persons, providing them with an illusory sense of purpose and ability. Mandatory, non-performance-based raises and promotions will also be offered to create a sense of upward mobility for even the most unremarkable, utterly replaceable employees.

The legislation also provides corporations with incentives to hire non-nabled workers, including tax breaks for those who hire one non-germane worker for every two talented hirees.

Finally, the Americans With No Abilities Act also contains tough new measures to prevent discrimination against the non-abled by banning prospective employers from asking such job-interview questions as, "What can you bring to this organization?" and "Do you have any special skills that would make you an asset to this company?"

"As a non-abled person, I frequently find myself unable to keep up with co-workers who have something going for them," said Mary Lou Gertz, who lost her position as an unessential filing clerk at a Minneapolis tile wholesaler last month because of her lack of notable skills. "This new law should really help people like me." With the passage of the Americans With No Abilities Act, Gertz and millions of other untalented, unessential citizens can finally see a light at the end of the tunnel.

Said Clinton: "It is our duty, both as lawmakers and as human beings, to provide each and every American citizen, regardless of his or her lack of value to society, some sort of space to take up in this great nation."

Subject: Agreement at the Summit

A squad of American soldiers was patrolling along the Iraqi border. They found the badly mangled dead body of an Iraqi soldier in a ditch along the road. A short distance up the road, they found a badly mangled American soldier in a ditch on the other side of the road. He was barely alive.

"What happened," a soldier asked.

"Well" he whispered, "I was walking down this road and ran into an Iraqi soldier. I looked him in the eye and yelled 'Hussein is an unprincipled, lying bastard.'"

"He looked me in the eye and shouted back, "Clinton is an unprincipled, lying bastard.'"

"We were standing in the middle of the road shaking hands when the truck hit us."

Gifts to intern: $149
Cuban cigars: $200
Legal defense: 3.7 million
Getting away with it all:

priceless

The new Platinum MasterCard has a
presidentially high spending limit so you
can get what you want out of life.

SLICK TIMES • 1-800-669-8444 • www.slick.com

Chapter Eight

THE X FILE

Subject: Three Gay Men

Three gay men died, and were going to be cremated. Their lovers happened to be at the funeral home at the same time, and were discussing what they planned to do with the ashes. The first man said, "My Benny loved to fly, so I'm going up in a plane and scatter his ashes in the sky." The second man said, "My Carl was a good fisherman, so I'm going to scatter his ashes in our favorite lake." The third man said, "My Jim was such a good lover, I think I'm going to dump his ashes in a pot of chili, so he can tear my ass up just one more time."

Subject: and you think your having a bad day . . .

A man was having problems with premature ejaculation, so
he decided to go to the doctor. He asked the doctor what he
could do to cure his problem. In response, the doctor said,
"When you feel like you are getting ready to ejaculate, try
startling yourself." That same day, the man went to the store
and bought himself a starter pistol. All excited to try this
suggestion, he ran home to his wife.

At home, he found his wife was in bed, naked and waiting. As the two began, they found themselves in the 69 position. The man, moments later, felt the sudden urge to ejaculate and fired the starter pistol.

The next day, the man went back to the doctor. The doctor asked, "How did it go?"

The man answered, "Not that well, when I fired the pistol, my wife shit on my face, bit 3 inches off my penis, and my
neighbor came out of the closet with his hands in the air."

Subject: Actual Article from the LA Times

"In retrospect, lighting the match was my big mistake. But I
was only trying to retrieve the gerbil," Eric Tomaszewski told
bemused doctors in the Severe Burn Unit of Salt Lake City
Hospital. Tomaszewski, and his homosexual partner Andrew
"Kiki" Farnum, had been admitted for emergency treatment
after a felching session had gone seriously wrong. "I pushed
a cardboard tube up his rectum and slipped Raggot, our
gerbil, in "he explained. "As usual, Kiki shouted out "Arma-
geddon", my cue that he'd had enough I tried to retrieve
Raggot but he wouldn't come out, so I peered into the tube
and struck a match, thinking the light might attract him." At
a hushed press conference, a hospital spokesman described
what happened next. "The match ignited a pocket of intestinal gas and a flame shot out of the tubing, igniting Mr.

Tomaszewski's hair and severely burning his face. It also set fire to the gerbil's fur and whiskers which in turn ignited a larger pocket of gas further up the intestine, propelling the rodent out like a cannonball." Tomaszewski suffered second degree burns and a broken nose from the impact of the gerbil, while Kiki Farnum suffered first and second degree burns to his anus and lower intestinal tract.

Subject: Serious analysis. PUSSY VS. BEER

- A beer is always wet. A pussy needs encouragement. Advantage: Beer
- A beer tastes horrible served hot. A pussy tastes better served hot. Advantage: Pussy
- Having an ice cold beer makes you satisfied. Having an ice cold pussy makes you Hillary Clinton. Advantage: Beer
- If you get a hair in your teeth consuming pussy, you are not disgusted. Advantage: Pussy
- 24 beers come in a box. A pussy is a box you can come in. Advantage: Pussy
- If you come home smelling like beer, your wife may get mad. If you come home smelling like pussy, she will *definitely* get mad. Advantage: Beer
- It is socially acceptable to have a beer in the stands at a football game. You are a legend if you have a pussy in the stands at a football game. Advantage: Pussy
- If a cop smells beer on your breath, you are going to get a breathalyzer. a cop smells pussy on your breath, you are going to get a high five. Advantage: Pussy
- With beer, bigger is better. Advantage: Beer
- Wearing a condom does not make a beer any less enjoyable. Advantage: Beer
- Pussy can make you see God. Beer can make you see the *porcelain* god. Advantage: Pussy

- If you think all day about the next pussy you will have, you are normal. If you think all day about your next beer, you are an alcoholic. Advantage: Pussy
- Peeling labels off of beers is fun. Peeling panties off of pussy is more fun. Advantage: Pussy
- If you suddenly drop a beer, it may break. If you suddenly drop a pussy, it may hunt you down like the dog that you are. Advantage: Beer
- If you change to another beer, your old brand will gladly have you back. Advantage: Beer
- The best pussy you have ever had is not gone once you have enjoyed it. Advantage: Pussy
- The worst pussy you have ever had is not gone once you have enjoyed it. Advantage: Beer
- The government taxes beer. Advantage: Pussy
- It's a close call, but the numbers never lie. Advantage: Pussy

Subject: Fairy Tales

Naughty Fairy Tales # 1
  Little Red Riding Hood was walking through the woods when suddenly the Big Bad Wolf jumped out from behind a tree and, holding a machete to Her throat, said, 'Red, I'm going to screw your brains out.' To that, Little Red Riding Hood calmly reached into her picnic basket and pulled out a . 44 magnum and pointed it at him and said, 'No you're not. You're going to eat me, just like it says in the book.

Naughty Fairy Tales # 2
  Pinocchio had a human girlfriend who would sometimes complain about splinters whenever they had sex. Pinocchio, therefore, went to visit Gepetto to see if he could help. Gepetto suggested he try a little sandpaper wherever indicated and Pinocchio skipped away enlightened. A couple of weeks later,

Gepetto saw Pinocchio bouncing happily through town and asked him, 'How's the girlfriend?' Pinocchio replied, 'Who needs a girlfriend?

Naughty Fairy Tales # 3

Snow White saw Pinocchio walking through the woods so she ran up behind him, knocked him flat on his back, and then sat on his face crying, 'Lie to me, Lie to me'

Naughty Fairy Tales # 4

Cinderella wants to go to the ball, but her wicked step-mother won't let her. As Cinderella sits crying in the garden, her fairy godmother appears, and promises to provide Cinderella with everything she needs to go to the ball, but only on two conditions. 'First, you must wear a diaphragm.' Cinderella agrees. 'What's the second 'You must be home by 2 a.m. Any later, and your diaphragm will turn into a pump-kin.' Cinderella agrees to be home by 2 a.m. The appointed hour comes and goes, and Cinderella doesn't show up. Fi-nally, at 5 a.m., Cinderella shows up, looking love-struck and **very** satisfied. 'Where have you been?' demands the fairy godmother. 'Your diaphragm was supposed to turn into a pumpkin three hours ago' 'I met a prince, Fairy Godmother. He took care of everything.' 'I know of no prince with that kind of power. Tell me his name' 'I can't remember, exactly . . . Peter Peter, something or other. . . .'

Naughty Fairy Tales #5

Mickey Mouse and Mini Mouse were in divorce court and the judge said to Mickey, 'You say here that your wife is crazy.' Mickey replied, 'No I didn't. I said she is fuckin' Goofy.'

Subject: Politically Correct

Canada and the state of Alaska have just passed laws making it an offence to use the word lesbian-in Canada they must now be called fur traders and in Alaska, klondykes. California is considering a similar law, referring to this minority as vagitarians.

Subject: Not a Member of NOW

A young Japanese girl had been taught all of her life that when she married she was to please her husband and never upset him. So the first morning of her honeymoon when the young Japanese bride crawled out of the bed after making love and she stooped down to pick up husband's clothes and she let a big fart. She looked up and said: "Excuse please, ' front hole so happy back hole whistle."

Subject: Blowjob Etiquette for Men

1-Women are under no obligation to perform this task

2-Extension of #1-be grateful

3-It is NOT standard operating procedure to cum on someone's face.

4-Extention to #3-we are not obligated to swallow.

5-My ears are not handles

6-Don't push on my head or I'll puke on your dick

7-NEVER FART

8-Just because I am having a period does not mean I will automatically blow you.

9-If I remove a pubic hair from my mouth, don't say I've wrecked it.

10-Don't turn on the TV right after you shoot.

11-It does not taste good-no protein jokes

12-Just because it's awake when you get up does not mean I have to kiss it" good morning."

Subject: Light my fire

A man who worked for the fire department came home and told his wife; "You know, we have a wonderful system at the fire department. Bell # 1 we all put our coats on. Bell # 2 rings, we all slide down the pole. Bell # 3 rings, we're on the truck ready to go.

From now on we are going to run this house the same way. When I say :Bell # 1, you strip naked. Bell #2, you jump into bed, and Bell # 3, we screw all night.

The next night, he comes home from work and yells: "Bell One!!" She takes off her clothes. Bell Two!!, she jumps into bed. "Bell Three!!" they begin to screw.

After two minutes, she yells: "Bell Four!!" what's bell four for? he asks. "More Hose! she says "You ain't nowhere near the fire!"

Subject: Ten Worst Pick Up Lines

10. Nice legs. What time do they open?
9. Do you work for UPS? I could have sworn you were checking out my package.
8. You've got 206 bones in you body, want one more?
7. Want to play army? I'll lay down and you can blow the hell out of me.
6. You can feel the magic between us. No, lower.
5. If it's true you are what you eat, I could be you by morning.
4. Those clothes would look great in a crumpled heap on my bedroom floor.
3. Do you sleep on your stomach at night? Can I?

2. Do you wash your panties in Windex because I can see myself in them.

And the Worst Pick Up Line is

1. (Looking down at crotch) It's not just going to suck itself.

Subject: He Broke the Code

A guy and his girl are about to go into his apartment. It's their third date. Before he can open the door, his girlfriend says, "I think I can tell how a man makes love by how he unlocks the door."

"Give me some examples", the guy replies.

"Well, if a guy shoves the key min the lock, and slams the door open, then that means he's a rough lover and not for me. If a man fumblers around with the key, that means he's inexperienced and that's a no-no also."

Then she says, coyly, "How do you unlock your door/"

"Well, first, I lick the lock."

Subject: Me First

A woman was in a coma. Nurses were giving her a bath. One of them touched her private area and noticed there was a response on the monitor. They went to her husband and explained what happened. "Crazy as it sounds, maybe a little oral sex may bring her out of the coma.."

The husband was skeptical but finally agreed. They closed the curtain for privacy.

After a few minutes the woman's monitor flat lined, no pulse, no heart rate. The nurses ran into the room.. The husband was standing there, pulling up his pants, and said, "I think she choked."

Subject: A Rose Would Smell as Sweet by Any Name

A fellow goes into a bar and meets a cute girl.
"What's your name," he says
"Carmen"
"That's nice," he says," is Carmen a family name?"
"No, I gave it to myself"
"Why," he asks.
"Because I like cars and men. What's your name?"
"Beer Fuck," he replies.

Chapter Nine

THE FIFTY BEST WEBSITES FOR HUMOR

ON THE INTERNET

If you believe the number of websites related to "Internet Humor" listed on the Infoseek search engine, there are 4,978,590 sites available for you to visit. I feel as if I stopped at almost all of them to come up with fifty sites that are truly amusing. Most of the sites related to humor are about as sharp as the leading edge of a BB.

Just a couple of words of advise. There is a lot of adult content throughout the Internet so use your judgement when sharing material. Also, websites improve, fail, adjust addresses or languish faster than Elizabeth's Taylor's weight changes. Today's penthouse may be tomorrow's outhouse. The order of this list is random. My # 1 may be your # 50.

www.cybercheese.com
3000 jokes, cartoons and stories.

www.thatsrich.com/
Stories, quotes, jokes, classic comedy, links

www.whyaduck.com
Marx Bros. Classic humor, film, outtakes

http://interactivespace.com/
Top ten lists, random thoughts

www.bl.net/forwards/
Amusing and annoying emails and chain letters

www.emailjoke.com
Jokes galore

www.wyomingvalley.com/jokebox/
Full of jokes including Clinton section

www.theonion.com/
Humorous spin on current news

www.unitedmedia.com/comics/dilbert
A classic look at business and large companies

www.netfunny.com/rhf/
6000 joke archive

www.comedy.com
Jokes, news with comic slant, audio from touring comedians

www.randomhouse.com/features/davebarry
Barry, a master humorist, in cyberspace

http://allworld.net/allworld/jokes.html/
Jokes and cartoons

www.menjokes.com/
Gender jokes and naughty cartoons

www.humorandjokes.com/
Adult humor, songs, cartoons, pictures + videos

www.scroom.com/humor/lawyer.html
Lawyer jokes

www.jokecentral.com/
Clean jokes

www.twistedhumor.com/
Adult jokes, pictures, audio, video

http://politicalhumor.about.com/entertainment/
    politicalhumor/
Topical political humor

www.golf-jokes.co.uk/
A funny look at a frustrating game

http://4allfree.com/
Fun spot for Webmasters to improve their site-free

http://lennyeliasatcomedyouthouse.com/
Satirical look at the news

www.happyshrink.com/
Laughter is the best medicine

www.solosier.com/womanbash/
Don't let your wife or girlfriend visit this site

www.startingpage.com/html/adult_humor.html
XXX humor-not for the faint of hear

www.republicanbay.com/humor/political-comedy.asp
Republican look at Washington with a collection of humor
    andsatire.

www.threestooges.com/
Great look at the genius of Larry, Moe and Curly

www.louisville.edu/~kprayb01/WC.html
The life and times of W. C. Fields

www.danielsen.com/jokes.shtml
Funniest Internet jokes and runners-up

www.yeeeoww.com/lampoon/lampoon.html
The Internet version of this irreverent magazine

www.ios.com/~critacco/farting.html
The classic farting contest held in the '30's between Paul
    Boomer of Australia and Lord Windesmere from En-
    gland. (**my favorite**).

www.jokesoup.com/officejokes.htm
Political, religious, office and courtship humor

www.graceweb.org/Laugh-A-Lot/
Clean jokes and humor

www.4point5.co.uk/
British humor-not for those easily offended.

www.netfunny.com/rhf/
Family and children's stories and jokes

www.funnyfunnypictures.com/
Audio and video clips

www.goofball.com/
Cartoons, jokes, videos, pictures and songs

www.bitchinbertha.com/
Cards can be sent to vent your anger or put a comic twist on
　　problems

http://crazyland.freeservers.com/
Pictures, toons, waves, links-Adult

www.tech-sol.net/humor/index.htm
Office humor

www.insults.net/
Insults for all occasions

http://artists.mp3s.com/artists/34/larry_weaver.html
Misheard/fractured song lyrics

www.ohyesuare.com/
Tremendous variety of humor and jokes

www.emtoo.org/humor/index.shtml
Clean comedy from Internet emails.

www.planetclick.com/cgi-bin/category.cgi?T=robin+williams
A vast array of Robin Williams films and comedy

www.laughmyassoff.com/
Adult humor

http://paulmerton.ox.ac.uk/
The best oxymoron site on the Internet

www.crapco.com/comedy/connection/
1,000 links to Internet humor sites

www.humorsearch.com/
Web search engine for all types of humor

www.dogpile.com
Web search engine for great humor sites

www.topjokes.com/
500 humor sites in database

www.dribbleglass.com
Great altered billboards

Happy surfing!!!

Although they restricted themselves to one drink at lunch time, Howard and Tom still found they were not at their most productive in the afternoons

Chapter Ten

HOW TO USE HUMOR TO YOUR

ADVANTAGE IN LIFE

Humor is a very valuable tool when dealing with friends, family, business associates or even strangers. Humor allows you to gain a rapport with whomever you are speaking and diffuse tension. Humor helps you gain acceptance and approval.

Here are some hints on how to use humor to your advantage:

File interesting ideas, stories, quips, etc. and use variations of this material in different circumstances. Plug in a phrase to bring humor to your point.
Don't just say it's hot out. Say it's hotter than two rabbits

making love in a wool sock in Birmingham, Alabama during July.

Share typical experiences and establish a rapport by participating in a common experience and placing your desired direction on the story.

Children are always saying funny things. While sitting on my lap, my granddaughter Kara said, "Do you ever brush your teeth." By sharing this story in a meeting, it broke the tension that existed, made me a real person with foibles and helped get our negotiations off to a friendly start. (I do brush my teeth.)

Take a few "one-liners", string them together to make a longer story, a fake news item or a funny twist on current issues.

A ventriloquist was making fun of the people of West Virginia through his dummy, Edgar. "West Virginians can't have driver's training class on Tuesday in High School because the car is being used for sex ed. training"

With that a West Virginian man jumped up and said, "Stop making those rude remarks about West Virginians." The ventriloquist said, I'm sorry, sir, I only wanted to amuse you. "The West Virginian countered, "Not you, it's that little fellow in your lap, Edgar, he's the rude one." (Actually two short stories combined)

Switch the setting of stories. Pick up the normal and place it in the abnormal.

—Mabuto, the great African chief was about to start his dinner when a fellow warrior said, "Mabuto, I don't like your brother-in-law."

Mabuto replied, "Well then, just eat the noodles."

*Invent topics-use the news-put an unusual twist on it.
—Hillary Clinton has prostate cancer.

Exaggerate similarities and differences, how people are alike and yet so diverse can be a great source of humor.
—A journalist speaking to a room full of Italian contractors in Detroit, Mi. at a convention said, "It feels funny being the only one in the room who doesn't know where Jimmy Hoffa is buried. (His legs are healing).

Definitions-define things by association or pun.
—Guru, n.—A computer owner who can read the manual.

Verse, limericks, short poems are easy to compose, can be used to make your point and not over-alienate anyone and can be very amusing.
If Johnny Cochran had represented Bill Clinton at his impeachment trail, his closing may have included the following:
• He cheats on his wife but that's his personal life.
• The economy's great, let the white boy skate.
• If the dress ain't a mess, he don't need to confess.
• If the sex is just oral, it's not really immoral.

Completely irrational stories with no hint of reality can relax even the most uptight group.
—At one time I was so fat that when I got on a scale that told your fortune, it read, "Come back when you are alone."

Wordplay, puns, double entendre, all these add spice to conversation.
Wife: "Your lodge meeting didn't last very long."
Husband: "The wife of the Grand Exalted, Invincible, Supreme Potentate made him stay home with the kids while she went shopping."

Insults can be exchanged that are all in fun. Self-effacing insults are effective also.

Two friends are at a party. One says, "This is a dull party, I think I'll go. "His pal says, "That'll help."

I once introduced the keynote speaker at a conference by saying we were schoolmates—when he was a senior, I was in first grade. The speaker took the rostrum and countered, "What few people know is that we are the same age."

Letters and emails written for humorous effect are great tools for laughter and to create a relaxed, positive atmosphere or to make your point without making an enemy.

Director, Billing Dept.
Shell Oil Co.

Dear Sir:
I have been a regular customer of Shell Oil and until recently, satisfied with your products and service.

On a recent trip, I stopped at the Lowell Reeds Shell Station in Arden, N.C.. Earlier in the day I had had a flat tire which the attendant at the Lowell Reeds station informed me he was unable to fix. I purchased a new tire and fifty miles down the highway, I had a blowout. Not a puncture nor a polite ladyfinger firecracker rupture but a howitzer blowout. It tore enough rubber from the tire to make sandals for a hippie commune. I was driving down I-85 at sixty miles an hour on three tires and one rim whose sound can be approximated by placing a handful of gravel and a young duck in a blender.

You can screw yourself with a cream cheese dildo if you entertain for one moment the delusion that I intend to pay for that tire.

Sincerely,

Humor is God's aspirin to soothe the headache of reality. Take at least one dose a day. For even greater relief, offer God's aspirin to a friend.